Start Your Own

OFFICE AND ADMINISTRATIVE SUPPORT SERVICE

Additional titles in *Entrepreneur's* **Startup Series**

Start Your Own

Entrepreneur
MAGAZINE'S

startup

Start Your Own

OFFICE AND ADMINISTRATIVE SUPPORT SERVICE

Your Step-by-Step Guide to Success

Entrepreneur Press and Courtney Thurman

EP
Entrepreneur.
Press

Editorial Director: Jere L. Calmes
Managing Editor: Marla Markman
Cover Design: Beth Hansen-Winter
Production and Composition: Eliot House Productions

This publication is designed to provide accurate and authoritative information in regard to the subject matter covered. It is sold with the understanding that the publisher is not engaged in rendering legal, accounting or other professional services. If legal advice or other expert assistance is required, the services of a competent professional person should be sought.

Library of Congress Cataloging-in-Publication Data
　　Thurman, Courtney.
　　　Start your own office and administrative support service/by Entrepreneur Press and Courtney Thurman.
　　　　p.　　cm.
　　　Includes index.
　　　ISBN-13: 978-1-59918-107-3 (alk. paper)
　　　ISBN-10: 1-59918-107-X (alk. paper)
　　　　1. Home-based business support services. I. Thurman, Courtney. II. Entrepreneur Press.

　　HD8039.B95S73 2007
　　651.068'1—dc22　　　　　　　　　　　　　　　　　　　　　　　　2007023255

Printed in Canada
12 11 10 09 08 07　　　　　　　　　　　　　　　　　　　　　　10 9 8 7 6 5 4 3 2 1

Contents

Preface

Business is becoming more complex every day, and the tools we use to run our companies are becoming increasingly sophisticated. This is creating tremendous opportunities for the business support services industry.

Other factors contributing to the growth of business support services include the increasing number of small businesses and homebased businesses, and the trend of outsourcing non-core business tasks. It just doesn't make sense for small companies to hire someone with every skill they need, especially when those skills are readily available from other small companies that specialize in various support-type services.

Consider a business that wants to send out a quarterly newsletter. It can purchase desktop-publishing software and a high-end laser printer and hire a staff writer and graphic designer (paying salary, benefits, etc.) to do what amounts to a few hours of work four times a year. Or they can contract with a business support services company to do a comparable job and pay only for the services they use. Which makes more sense?

Maybe a business needs tapes transcribed. Should it hire a typist and buy transcription equipment, or send the tapes out to a service that can do it for them? Or what about when a business has a short-term special project that needs to be done but doesn't have the staff available to do it? Should it hire for the short term or outsource to a business support service? And then there's the homebased business owner who needs administrative work done but doesn't have the physical space to hire someone to come in and work, even on a part-time basis—a business support service company may be the answer.

Small businesses are not the only customers of business support services. Large corporations also regularly use them to outsource routine tasks and special projects. Individuals are also a substantial customer group: students who need term papers typed; job seekers who need professional-looking resumes; writers who need help with typing, editing, and manuscript preparation; and more. Given this variety of potential clients, a business support service firm can successfully operate in just about any part of the country and in communities of all sizes.

Another lure of the business support service industry is the diversity it offers operators. You determine your hours and your specialty or you can offer a wide range of services from basic word processing to database management to desktop publishing. You can earn a comfortable income working from home as a solo operator, or you can set up in a commercial location with employees. The main requirement of this industry is the quality of your work and the dedication you have to improving your craft. Although this is an easy-to-enter industry, you will soon find the difference between the business support services that are thriving and those that are not.

Regardless of the particular type of business services you want to start, this book will tell you how to do it. We'll start with an overview of the industry, look at the services you'll want to consider offering, and then go through the step-by-step process of setting up and running your new venture.

Be prepared; when you finish this book, you should be well-equipped with what it takes to make this a prosperous and long-lasting career!

Much More
than Typing

The business support service industry has changed radically in the past several years, and many of the entrepreneurs we've interviewed said that the business they built originally looks almost nothing like what it has become. Even more, each one had difficulty forecasting how the industry will change in the next 10 years because it is so dynamic. We surveyed 40 members of the Alliance for Virtual Businesses and interviewed a few of them further so we could give you current information, feedback, and statistics about how they entered the industry, built their business, and how they continue to tailor their services and skills to make their businesses thrive.

There are many terms for this type of business from "administrative support services," "office support services," and for many, "virtual assisting services." No matter what title you apply to this business, it still doesn't fully explain the vast scope of services you can offer since these businesses now offer everything from desktop publishing, web design, and many more sophisticated and talented service packages. Given the growth of the industry in the past several years and the trends for even greater growth, it's easy to assume that the more flexible you are in your ability to customize your services, the better you will do.

The size of the market for business support services is difficult to estimate for a number of reasons—primarily because the U.S. Bureau of the Census mixes other types of businesses with business support services. Also, the providers, services, and customers are constantly evolving with technological advances. Many of our surveyed experts are talking about using remote desktop access to conduct virtual meetings, using Voice-over IP to teleconference, and utilizing online meeting rooms and online conferences.

Keep in mind that this is a professional service business and your services are always going to be needed. Depending on your specialty, seasonal fluctuations may vary, but if you offer a portfolio of services, most likely one service demand will complement a slowdown in another. We will cover the vast variety of services you can offer and think about which services will balance each other and how you can gain the knowledge and training necessary to truly be a specialist in each area.

As a business support service owner, be prepared for the reality that the company you start today will likely bear little resemblance to the one you'll be running in the future. Sharon Williams, chairperson for the Alliance for Virtual Businesses gives the following four forecasts for the industry in the next five to ten years:

1. Business support services entrepreneurs will begin standardized training and certification programs making them more widely accepted among professional organizations and throughout the industry.

2. The industry will receive greater recognition and acceptance as a viable and cost-effective alternative to on-site staffing.

3. Business support service owners with mediocre skills will realize the demand in the industry that requires tech-savvy and highly-trained experts.

4. Savvy service owners will continue their education, increase their familiarity with new and changing technologies, and develop targeted marketing strategies to educate ideal clients.

As long as you pay attention to what's going on in the market, stay flexible, and continue to educate yourself on new technologies, your chances of having a strong, profitable operation are excellent.

Industry Trends

Let's look further into the trends for this industry from some successful owners. Sharon says that "savvy [owners] are breaking new ground and educating the business community about the advantages and benefits of partnering with them. As a result, the industry is exploding. More and more industries are aware of outsourcing and demand highly trained and qualified service providers.

Since external and intra-industry awareness is evolving, service owners, individually and as part of organized media and promotion campaigns, must keep up with increasing demand. Currently, there are unlimited opportunities for business growth and development. I expect this trend to continue for years to come."

She explains that "virtual assisting and outsourcing is a relatively new industry. Since its origin in the mid-1990s, more than 20,000 professional office support staff located around the globe have transitioned into savvy business owners. I recommend that newcomers considering this industry as a viable business opportunity take advantage of much of the resources, education, and networking offered, as it will aid in their development and ultimate business growth and success."

Sherry Watkins says that the industry has changed a lot since she's been in business. "Four years ago when I first started watching the industry, many people were hesitant of hiring someone they could not meet in person. Today, more and more businesses are realizing that they can get the expertise without the face-to-face, and this offers them freedom from the hassles of being an employer on top of trying to do their business. Now they are not limited to the work force in their local communities. I see a surge of growth coming in the next five to ten years as more entrepreneurs take advantage of the technology and freedom this industry offers. We too are no longer limited to our local communities."

"I think the industry will become increasingly more computerized."

—Gay Lynn Kirsch, Executive Secretarial Services, LLC

Is It In You?

Who is likely to start a business support service company? Many of today's owners were employees doing similar tasks for other

Trend Analysis Checklist

To track emerging trends that can affect small businesses in general and your business in particular, you need to stay informed.

❑ Read a major metropolitan newspaper, as well as one or two papers serving your local community. This way, you can stay informed on current events on both local and global scales.

❑ Join associations that serve your industry. To find an appropriate association, consult the *Encyclopedia of Associations*, published by Gale Research. You can find this publication in larger libraries.

❑ Keep track of bestselling nonfiction books. Although these books may not always apply directly to your business, they may reveal trends that you can use to your advantage.

❑ Contact government agencies or consult government publications for industry-specific information. The departments of Commerce and Labor as well as the Census Bureau, for instance, have data tracking various industry trends. You might also consult large libraries (particularly those in large public universities) for information gathered by the government. Such libraries often have sections devoted to government publications.

❑ Contact manufacturers, wholesalers and distributors serving your industry. They can furnish information on their products and on market research they may have done.

❑ If you have access to an online information service, you might be able to find a source of the latest information on your industry.

❑ Subscribe to relevant trade periodicals and newsletters. Many trade associations publish periodicals, which are usually filled with valuable management tips, industry trends, buying guides, etc.

❑ Attend industry conventions and inventor trade shows. These venues offer an exciting array of information regarding specific industries as well as new product ideas.

❑ Read journals and magazines on a local as well as national level that deal with small-business or business in general. Publications like the *Wall Street Journal* and *Entrepreneur* are valuable sources of trends that are developing on a national scale, and of detailed information on specific business opportunities. Local business journals that cover key developments in your own community are also important because you can track new ideas and trends that appeal to a specific geographic market.

Check out more checklists like these at Entrepreneur.com.

companies and saw the opportunity to be in business for themselves. Some wanted full-time businesses; others were looking for a solid part-time income source. Most saw the demand in the industry and have found it a rewarding experience. Even more, they saw that by becoming an expert at those services, they could surpass their competition and gain loyal clients. Do you have the resolve to craft your skills and become an entrepreneur?

Next we'll show you some of the start-up stories from some of our surveyed entrepreneurs, and although their businesses vary by location and services provided, the common thread among these operators is that they all did the type of work involved before they actually began running their own company. This explains one of the biggest challenges of starting and running a business support service: the need to go beyond pure technical skills and experience and understand how to manage and grow a business.

Start-Up Stories

Charlene Davis had been a full-time legal assistant when she started her part-time homebased business in Florida. Her goal was to have more time and flexibility to be at home with her newly-adopted son, but to not completely give up her career and income. In fact, one of her key challenges is keeping her business part-time and small. "I could easily turn it into a big business because I've gotten a lot of referrals and I turn down a lot of work," she says. "Fortunately, I don't [need] the income, and I prefer to keep my hours light. I choose when and when not to work, and I keep my client list very short and manageable."

Sharon Williams tells that she was "downsized from government employment and promised [myself] that no one would ever determine if I received a paycheck again. I saved a date and opened my business doors without having one client and said, 'I can do this.' I have since built a successful international practice."

Diana Ennen started her business to be with her son. "He went to daycare for three weeks and I just knew it wasn't for me, having others raise him and spend more time with him than me. I also knew I could do better than working at the medical office I was at. I practically ran that office and after two years, I received a small 25-cent raise. I knew I was worth more. Plus, I was tired of being someone's secretary."

For Gay Lynn Kirsch, this was her second homebased business. She had started one in South Carolina that she ran part-time while working a full-time job. She then came to the DC area and was working full-time when she was laid off while pregnant and after she had her baby, decided to reopen the business in her new area.

Janice Byer says, "I ran my father's company from my home and when he retired, I knew that I didn't want to go back out to work. I wanted to work from home. It just

Self-Assessment Worksheet

Use this self-assessment worksheet to see if working for yourself is right for you. After you've completed all the questions, look for a pattern in the answers. For example, do you see a need for your services and skills in areas where you excel?

○ List at least five things you like to do or excel in at work:

1. _____
2. _____
3. _____
4. _____
5. _____

○ List at least five things you don't like or areas where you need to improve at work:

1. _____
2. _____
3. _____
4. _____
5. _____

○ List three services that would make your life easier at work:

1. _____
2. _____
3. _____

○ When people ask you what you do, what's your answer? _____

_____

○ List three things you enjoy about your work:

1. _____
2. _____
3. _____

Self-Assessment Worksheet, continued

○ List three things you dislike about your work:

1. _____

2. _____

3. _____

○ When people tell you what they like most about you, they say: _____

_____

○ Some people dislike the fact that you: _____

_____

○ Other than your main occupation, list any other skills you possess, whether you excel at them or not: _____

_____

_____

○ In addition to becoming more financially independent, you would also like to become more: _____

_____

_____

○ List at least three things you would like to improve about your personal life:

1. _____

2. _____

3. _____

○ List three things you think need to be improved in your industry:

1. _____

2. _____

3. _____

Adapted from *Entrepreneur* Magazine's *Start Your Own Business*.

felt right to me. Not to mention, I had a very young daughter at the time and couldn't imagine going back out to work and putting her in daycare."

Lyn Prowse-Bishop said her reasons were "a combination of needing the money and wanting to be available to my new child. I was on 12 months maternity leave from my full-time job. Maternity leave is unpaid in my field at the current time. Six months in, I found I needed to return to work because the money ran out and my husband's salary was not enough to cover all of our expenses. I approached my boss with the suggestion that I return to work six months early if he could be flexible and have me for only two days a week onsite and work remotely the other three and had even drafted a proposal. He was not at all interested and said I should return at the end of my 12 months. I then went out and got a job share role in a law firm working two days a week and pursued the idea of working from home for myself. Within 6 months, I had discovered niche marketing and had my first client. Within 12 months, I had three clients. By 18 months, I was working full-time at home."

Sherry Watkins wanted to get rid of her commute. "Five years ago when my husband and I purchased our home, we set a goal to eliminate the 60 mile one-way commute in five years. The growth in technology has literally wiped away the necessity to commute, combined with the fact that I had a back injury last summer

Sit this One Out

If you have small children and you're starting a homebased business support service, don't try to do it without a sitter. You won't be able to concentrate on your work if you're also listening for the kids. To be fair to yourself, your company, your clients, and your children, arrange for someone to watch them while you're working and meeting with clients.

"You can always run errands with the children in tow—it may take longer, but it's not a real hardship," says Charlene. "But when you're actually working on projects, you need time to do it uninterrupted, when you can really focus on the job itself."

Keep in mind that if you're going to be at home working within earshot of the kids, you can hire a younger, less experienced, less expensive sitter than you might hire if you were going to be out.

and the commute became too much. We've met our goal and now we don't need to commute."

Lanel Taylor started a business because of the need for the services and autonomy. "I was going back to school and needed something flexible to allow me to work around my school schedule. I continued with it after I graduated because of the need for my services and I liked what I'm doing."

Carol Deckert needed the income but found that she was overqualified for many administrative positions. "The company employing me at the time went out of business and I was told by the Unemployment Bureau that my skills were too advanced to be an administrative assistant. I then began working for myself as a secretarial services owner, now known as a virtual assistant. I have now found my niche as a Virtual Marketing Assistant."

Lisa Wells has a bit of a different story. "My husband received military orders to move from Camp Pendleton, California, to Camp Lejeune, North Carolina. The job market in North Carolina was extremely tight for my position as an IT Specialist. So I decided to start my own business."

Wendy Weightman had numerous reasons to start her own business. "I needed the extra money in addition to my husband's income but wanted to work part-time on my own terms and have flexible hours to achieve a better work/life balance. I also wanted to save on time and costs of being an employee, such as two hours commuting each day, expensive work clothes, bought lunches, getting home and cooking dinner late, reducing family stress at the end of the day, and helping my teenagers with homework problems, etc. I had wanted to work from home for years and finally finding out about the industry on the internet made it easy for me to get connected and start my business—my dream job!"

Joann Voss began doing transcribing for court reporters at night to supplement her income from her full-time office manager's job. "I became overwhelmed with how much outside work I was getting, so I quit my job and started doing this full time," she says. That was in 1984; today, her company, Voss Transcriptions specializes in audiotape and videotape transcription, and does work for clients across the country.

Bill Pypes' path to owning a business support service was less traditional. His wife actually started the business he now runs in Iowa. She was successfully working from home, and after their second child was born, Bill began helping her while he attended graduate school. When their third child came along, she opened a homebased daycare center, and Bill took over the business support service and moved it into a commercial office.

Each business owner has a different story, but of our forty survey participants, most of them looked at this industry because they either saw a need for their services, needed the extra income, wanted the autonomy, wanted to stay at home with their

▲

children, or had other motivations, but each has worked hard to make it a success and have met their goals.

The Sky's the Limit

To understand the future potential, take a look at how the industry has evolved. Over the past decade, the administrative demands of doing business have grown tremendously, creating a need for experienced support. With the advent of complex computer systems and increasingly sophisticated software and online capabilities, the skill and knowledge requirements of business support owners have also increased. The newest technologies today, according to the Alliance for Virtual Businesses are VoIP, whiteboarding, webcams, video podcasting, and online meeting rooms. Furthermore, they foresee autoresponders, PDAs, and iPods becoming more integral to the daily functions of the business support service industry. Sharon Williams of the Alliance says that, "The influx and standardization of web-based secured and encrypted sites has revolutionized the transcription industry as [business support service owners] now offer online, secured, digital dictation, and transcription services. Administrative support services and time accountability software can be tracked and reviewed by team

Profit Prophet

A business support service is not a get-rich-quick operation. Like most legitimate businesses, it takes dedication, hard work, and a lot of time to build a profitable company. But with a well-thought-out, enthusiastic marketing plan, you'll probably see your income exceed your cumulative expenses three to 12 months after opening your doors. How much you'll ultimately make depends on how hard you're willing to work, how many hours you put in, and the type of business you start (small, one-person shop, or larger operation with employees).

If you work alone, keep in mind that you'll only be able to bill about 75 percent of your available business hours—the rest of your time will be spent marketing, doing your own administrative work, and on other non-billable tasks. And even though you can get "out of the red" fairly quickly in this business, it could take a year or more before you are actually working full time on clients' projects.

members. [Now you] can share client desktops via access software such as GotoMyPC and PCAnywhere. [Owners] meet with clients in interactive meeting rooms, equipped with whiteboarding and VoIP capabilities. As a result of the influence of these innovative technologies, client information is easily accessible and the services are more accountable and marketable."

At the same time, the general business landscape has changed dramatically. Big businesses are looking for ways to streamline their operations, and one popular option is outsourcing, where they retain another company to provide a service that may have traditionally been done by employees. Small companies want to stay lean and profitable, so they, too, are turning to outsourcing, rather than fattening up their payrolls.

Combine the obvious need with the new way of operating in the business world, and you have a dynamic young industry wide-open with opportunity: business support services. In fact, even though there is so much opportunity, if you don't have a clear plan, specific services, and a target market, your chances of success are slim. But with a lot of thought and preparation, and a minimal amount of cash, you can quickly be on the road to profitability.

2

Making the Choice

Owning a business support service doesn't necessarily require building the company from scratch. You might want to consider buying an existing business, especially if the appeal of being in business for yourself is in running the company rather than starting it.

Beware!
Don't be a victim of a scam. You'll see plenty of ads out there that promise you can make lots of money working from home on your computer. Sadly, many of these offers are scams that ask you to send money you'll never recoup. Be a smart consumer: If something sounds too good to be true, it probably is.

This alternative route to business ownership has some advantages worth considering. It allows you to bypass all the steps involved in creating a business infrastructure because the original owner has already done that. You can take over an operation that is already generating cash flow—and perhaps even profits. You'll have a history on which to build your forecasts and a future that includes an established customer base. Also, you'll have had all the procedures and policies in place so you won't have to work through those issues alone. And there's generally less risk involved in buying an existing concern than there is in creating a whole new company and financing is typically easier because lenders like to see a proven track record.

Of course, there are drawbacks to buying a business. Though the actual dollar amounts depend on the size and type of business, it often takes more cash to buy an existing business than to start one yourself. When you buy a company's assets, you'll usually get stuck with at least some of the liabilities. And it's highly unlikely that you'll find an existing business that is precisely the company you would have built on your own. Even so, you just might find that the business you want is currently owned by someone else.

Why do people sell businesses—especially profitable ones? For a variety of reasons. Many entrepreneurs are happiest during the start-up and early growth stages of a company; once the business is running smoothly they get bored and begin looking for something new. Other business owners may grow tired of the responsibility, or be facing health or other personal issues that motivate them to sell their companies. In fact, some of the most successful entrepreneurs go into business with a solid plan for how they're going to get out of the business when the time comes.

When looking for a business to buy, make sure you have a good idea of what you're looking for. How many employees should it have? How many miles from your home can it be? If you decide to shop around for an existing business support service, look at every service provider in the area that meets your requirements; just because it isn't on the market doesn't mean it isn't for sale. Use your networking skills

Smart Tip *Tip...*
Check out www.bizbuy sell.com if you are looking for a business to buy, need broker to help you along the way, or you want to get involved with a franchise. It also has great tips on business valuation and financing.

to find potential companies; let friends and colleagues know what you're looking for. Start by checking out your local newspaper's classified ad section under "Business Opportunities" or "Businesses For Sale." You might even consider placing a "wanted to buy" classified ad.

Evaluating a Company

One of the most challenging financial calculations is figuring out what a business is worth. You may want to take the time to research the selling price and terms of recently sold companies in the industry, and use them as a guide. Or you may value the company based on its after-tax cash flow, or on the value of the company's assets, if they were liquidated, minus the debts and liabilities. You should call on your financial advisors to assist you with working through these calculations.

The figures are only part of the equation. Elements that are not as easy to assign a value to include the company's reputation and the strength of the relationship the current owner has with customers and employees.

Thorough due diligence is an essential part of the acquisition process. Be aware that purchasing a company takes a lot more than just signing a contract and writing a check. The amount of research and due diligence is sizable and you need to review everything from tax returns, loan compliance, customer satisfaction, cash flow, supplier contracts, and more. Remember that you have the right and the responsibility to know exactly what you are buying and from whom. If you don't do enough research before buying the company, it's usually too late to avoid problems and possible financial losses. You should have a team of experts to assist you in the valuation process. Have your accountant assist you in evaluating the financial statements and tax issues, your banker help with financing issues, and your attorney guide you in reviewing contracts, corporate status, and other legal concerns. Don't forget that you want an expert to assist you with personnel if the company has employees and a sales and marketing expert to assess the marketing strength and customer service health of the company.

So after you have had your team assess the current standing of the company, how do you agree on a purchase price? The best information for determining the value of the company is the present value of future cash flows, which is how much the business will bring in. To start, have your accountant prepare forecasted financial statements for the next five years and analyze the current cash available compared to the

Smart Tip

Tip...

If you buy an existing business support service, include a non-compete clause in your terms of sale; your new business won't be worth much if the seller opens a rival operation down the street a few weeks after you take over the old company.

Business Evaluation Checklist

Use this extensive checklist to make sure you get answers to all your important questions before you purchase a business.

❑ Why does the current owner want to sell the business? _____

❑ What type of growth potential does this business have? _____

❑ If the business is in decline, will you be able to save it and make it successful? __

_____

❑ Is the business in sound financial condition? _____

_____

❑ Have you seen audited year-end financial statements for the business? Have you reviewed the most recent statements? Have you reviewed the business's last five tax returns? _____

❑ Have you seen copies of all of the business's current contracts? _____

❑ Have you planned any sales promotions? _____

❑ Have you planned a publicity campaign? _____

❑ Is the business now, or has it ever been, under investigation by any government agency? If so, what is the status of any current investigation? What were the results of any past investigation? _____

❑ Is the business currently involved in a lawsuit, or has it ever been involved in one? If so, what is the status or result? _____

❑ Does the business have any debts or liens against it? If so, what are they for, and in what amounts? _____

❑ What percentage of the business's accounts are past due? How much does the business write off each year for bad debts? _____

❑ How many customers does the business serve on a regular basis? _____

❑ Who makes up the market for this business? Where are your customers located?

❑ Does the amount of business vary from season to season? _____

❑ Does any single customer account for a large portion of the sales volume? If so, would the business be able to survive without this customer? Remember, the larger the customer base is, the more easily you will be able to survive the loss of any customers. If, on the other hand, the business exists mainly to serve a single client, the loss of that client could be catastrophic. _____

❑ How does the business market its business support services? Does its competition use the same methods? If not, what methods does the competition use? How successful are they? _____

Business Evaluation Checklist, continued

❑ Does the business have exclusive rights to market any particular services? If so, how has it obtained this exclusively? Is it making the best possible use of this exclusivity? Do you have written proof that the current business owner can transfer this exclusivity to you? _____

❑ What competition does the business face? How can the business compete successfully? Have the business' competitors changed recently? Have any of them gone out of business, for instance? _____

_____

❑ Does the business have all the equipment necessary? Will you need to add or update any equipment? _____

_____

❑ What is the business' current inventory worth? Will you be able to use any of this inventory, or is it inconsistent with your intended service offerings? _____

_____

❑ How many employees does the business have? What positions do they hold? __

_____

❑ Does the business pay its employees high wages, or are the wages average or low?

_____

❑ Does the business experience high employee turnover? If so, why? _____

_____

❑ What benefits does the business offer its employees? _____

_____

❑ Will the change of ownership cause any changes in personnel? _____

_____

❑ Which employees are the most important to the company? _____

_____

❑ Do any of the business's employees belong to any unions?

_____

Excerpted and adapted from Entrepreneur.com on *How to Buy a Business*.

▲

business debt. Your accountant can help you assess the risk of buying this business and determine if it's a better value to buy a business versus starting your own. And remember that you can walk away from the deal at any point in the negotiation process before a contract is signed.

Things to Consider When Buying a Business

The following is a list of items to consider verifying for the value of the business you are looking to buy. It is excerpted and adapted from Entrepreneur.com on *How to Buy a Business.*

1. *Inventory.* Refers to all products and materials inventoried for resale or use in servicing a client. Important note: You or a qualified representative should be present during any examination of inventory. You should know the status of inventory, what's on hand at present, and what was on hand at the end of the last fiscal year and the one preceding that. You should also have the inventory appraised. After all, this is a hard asset and you need to know what dollar value to assign it. What is its quality? What condition is it in? Keep in mind that you don't have to accept the value of this inventory: it is subject to negotiation.

2. *Furniture, fixtures, equipment, and building.* This includes all products, office equipment, and assets of the business. Get a list from the seller that includes the name and model number of each piece of equipment. Then determine its present condition, market value when purchased versus present market value, and whether the equipment was purchased or leased. Find out how much the seller has invested in leasehold improvements and maintenance in order to keep the facility in good condition. Determine what modifications you'll have to make to the building or layout in order for it to suit your needs.

3. *Copies of all contracts and legal documents.* Contracts would include all lease and purchase agreements, distribution agreements, subcontractor agreements, sales contracts, union contracts, employment agreements, and any other instruments used to legally bind the business. Also, evaluate all other legal documents such as fictitious business name statements, articles of incorporation, registered trademarks, copyrights, patents, etc. In the case of a real-estate lease, you need to find out if it is transferable, how long it runs, its terms, and if the landlord needs to give his or her permission for assignment of the lease.

4. *Incorporation.* If the company is a corporation, check to see what state it's registered in and whether it's operating as a foreign corporation within its own state.

5. *Tax returns for the past five years.* Many small business owners make use of the business for personal needs. They may buy products they personally use and charge them to the business or take vacations using company funds, go to trade shows with their spouses, etc. You have to use your analytical skills and those of your accountant to determine what the actual financial net worth of the company is.

6. *Financial statements for the past five years.* Evaluate these statements, including all books and financial records, and compare them to their tax returns. This is especially important for determining the earning power of the business. The sales and operating ratios should be examined with the help of an accountant familiar with the type of business you are considering. The operating ratios should also be compared against industry ratios which can be found in annual reports produced by Robert Morris & Associates as well as Dun & Bradstreet.

7. *Sales records.* Although sales will be logged in the financial statements, you should also evaluate the monthly sales records for the past 36 months or more. Break sales down by product categories if several products are involved, as well as by cash and credit sales. This is a valuable indicator of current business activity and provides some understanding of cycles that the business may go through. Compare the industry norms of seasonal patterns with what you see in the business. Also, obtain the sales figures of the ten largest accounts for the past 12 months. If the seller doesn't want to release his or her largest accounts by name, it's fine to assign them a code. You're only interested in the sales pattern.

8. *Complete list of liabilities.* Consult an independent attorney and accountant to examine the list of liabilities to determine potential costs and legal ramifications. Find out if the owner has used assets such as capital equipment or accounts receivable as collateral to secure short-term loans, if there are liens by creditors against assets, lawsuits, or other claims. Your accountant should also check for unrecorded liabilities such as employee benefit claims, out-of-court settlements being paid off, etc.

9. *All accounts receivable.* Break them down by 30 days, 60 days, 90 days, and beyond. Checking the age of receivables is important because the longer the period they are outstanding, the lower the value of the account. You should also make a list of the top ten accounts and check their creditworthiness. If the clientele is creditworthy, and the majority of the accounts are outstanding beyond 60 days, a stricter credit collections policy may speed up the collection of receivables.

10. *All accounts payable.* Like accounts receivable, accounts payable should be broken down by 30 days, 60 days, and 90 days. This is important in determining how well cash flows through the company. On payables more than 90 days old,

▲

you should check to see if any creditors have placed a lien on the company's assets.

11. *Debt disclosure*. This includes all outstanding notes, loans, and any other debt to which the business has agreed. See, too, if there are any business investments on the books that may have taken place outside of the normal area. Look at the level of loans to customers as well.

13. *Customer patterns*. If this is the type of business that can track customers, you will want to know specific characteristics concerning current customers, such as: How many are first-time clients? How many customers were lost over the past year? When are the peak buying seasons for current customers? What type of service is the most popular?

14. *Marketing strategies*. How does the owner obtain customers? Does he or she offer discounts, advertise aggressively, or conduct public-relations campaigns? You should get copies of all sales literature to see the kind of image that is being projected by the business. When you look at the literature, pretend that you are a customer being solicited by the company. How does it make you feel? This can give you some idea of how the company is perceived by its market.

15. *Advertising costs*. Analyze advertising costs. It is often better for a business to postpone profit at year-end until the next year by spending a lot of money on advertising during the last month of the fiscal year.

16. *Price checks*. Evaluate current price lists and discount schedules for all services, the date of the last price increase, and the percentage of increase. You might even go back and look at the previous price increase to see what percentage it was and determine when you are likely to be able to raise prices, and in the business support service industry; rates. Here again, compare what you see in the business you are looking at, with standards in the industry. Are they charging the rates that you would charge?

17. *Industry and market history*. You should analyze the industry as well as the specific market segments of the business targets. You need to find out if sales in the industry, as well as in the market segment, have been growing, declining, or have remained stagnant. This is very important to determine future profit potential.

18. *Location and market area*. Evaluate the location of the business and the market area surrounding it. You should conduct a thorough analysis of the business's location and the trading areas surrounding the location including economic outlook, demographics, and competition. For service businesses, get a map of the area covered by the business. Find out, based on the locations of various accounts, if there are any special requirements for delivering the product, or

any transportation difficulties encountered by the business in getting the product to market.

19. *Reputation of the business.* The image of the business in the eyes of customers and suppliers is extremely important. As we mentioned, the image of the business can be an asset, or a liability. Interview customers, suppliers, and the bank, as well as the owners of other businesses in the area, to determine the reputation of the business.

20. *Seller-customer ties.* You must find out if any customers are related or have any special ties to the present owner of the business. How long has any such account been with the company? What percentage of the company's business is accounted for by this particular customer or set of customers? Will this customer continue to purchase from the company if the ownership changes?

21. *Inflated salaries.* Some salaries may be inflated or perhaps the current owner may have a relative on the payroll who isn't working for the company. All of these possibilities should be analyzed.

22. *List of current employees and organizational chart.* Current employees can be a valuable asset, especially key personnel. Evaluate the organizational chart to understand who is responsible to whom. You must also look at the management practices of the company and know the wages of all employees and their length of employment. Examine any management-employee contracts that exist aside from a union agreement, as well as details of employee benefit plans; profit-sharing; health, life and accident insurance; vacation policies; and any employee-related lawsuits against the company.

23. *Occupational Safety and Health Administration (OSHA) requirements.* Find out if the facility meets all occupational safety and health requirements and whether it has been inspected. If you feel that the seller is "hedging" on this and you see some things you feel might not be safe on the premises, you can ask OSHA to help you with an inspection. As a prospective buyer of a business that may come under OSHA scrutiny, you need to be certain that you are not buying an unsafe business. Some sellers may perceive your asking for OSHA's help as a dirty trick. But you must realize that as a prospective, serious buyer, you need to protect your position.

24. *Insurance.* Establish what type of insurance coverage is held for the operation of the business and all of its properties as well as who the underwriter and local company representative is, and how much the premiums are. Some businesses are underinsured and operating under potentially disastrous situations in case of fire or a major catastrophe. If you come into an underinsured operation, you could be wiped out if a major loss occurs.

▲

Going It on Your Own

Although buying an existing business may be a good way to enter the industry, most business support service owners start their own companies. This way, you can choose the exact services you want to offer, define the market you want to serve, and do things your way from the start. Now let's assess your goals and start planning your new venture.

Plan
First

So you are thinking that you are ready to get your business started, but the first and possibly the most important step is your plan. What made you want to join this industry? Did you notice a trend of outside work at your current job and see a need for your services? Did a friend tell you it was a lucrative business?

Motivation

Assess your motivations for starting this business using the Personal Goals Worksheet on page 25. Granted, you may launch a very successful small business, but it will take time and hard work to get you a full book of business and a steady work flow.

Make a list of your goals. Do you want a part-time home business or a full-time service company? If you are successful, what does "success" look like for you? Are you running a fast-paced office of five employees or are you making enough money to work three days a week in your pajamas? List what you want as an end result and structure your business plan to get you there, which we will discuss later.

Stat Fact

We interviewed 40 business support service entrepreneurs and 53 percent reported that they work 25 to 40 hours a week. Thirty-five percent claim to work up to 60 hours a week but much of it consists of working on their business as much as their support service projects.

Influence

Next, do an "influence check." Who is going to influence your decisions? Who already has influenced you? Are you relying on a friend already in the industry to give you your inside track? Do you have a mentor lined up to help you along the way?

Many entrepreneurs do almost all of the research themselves, but it's better to get a coach, trainer or mentor to speed you past the roadblocks that will inevitably arise. Be careful, just because the advice is free doesn't mean it's the best—sometimes it's better to pay for a coach or mentor who can help you with the most important decisions.

Contribution

Here's a tough question: What are you willing to contribute? Make a list of what you are going to give to the business in terms of time, personal space, and resources.

Stat Fact

In 2006, there were 800 Service Corp or Retired Executives (SCORE) offices nationwide with over 10,000 counselors available to help.

We will cover financial start-up costs in Chapter 9, but your contribution to the business will be much greater than just money.

Are you going to dedicate part of your home to make a home office? Can you be on-call for your clients? Most business support services are contacted last minute and need rush jobs—can you dedicate yourself to that schedule? If not, let's build your business plan so that you can structure your business model to fit to your contribution list.

Personal Goals Worksheet

To accomplish professional or personal goals, you need to lay out a roadmap for yourself. Come back to this worksheet on a regular basis since your goals may change and you will want to track your progress.

○ When people tell you what they like most about you, they say: _____

_____

○ Being an entrepreneur is important to me because: _____

_____

○ What I like best about working for myself is: _____

_____

○ In five years, I would like my business to be: _____

_____

_____

○ When I look back over the past five years of my career, I feel: _____

_____

_____

○ My financial situation now is: _____

_____

○ I feel like the next step I must take with my business is: _____

_____

○ The most important part of my business is (or will be): _____

_____

○ The area of my business I really need to excel in is: _____

_____

Adapted from *Entrepreneur* Magazine's *Start Your Own Business.*

If you assess your motivations, goals, and what you are willing to contribute to the business, writing your business plan will be much easier and will minimize surprises down the road.

Sharon Williams gives these 14 recommendations for business support service entrepreneurs just starting out:

1. *Develop a strong business plan*, with specific short and long term goals.

2. *Create a marketing strategy.*

3. *Consult a mentor or coach.*

4. *Create an advocates group*, individuals who believe in you and will help promote your business.

5. *Set aside rainy day funds*—minimally a 60 day nest egg to cover your expenses of daily living.

6. *Solicit family support*; explain your business concept and how they can assist by respecting that you work from home, as they respect others who work in brick-and-mortar businesses.

7. *Reward yourself.* Whenever you achieve a goal, be it weekly, large, or small, celebrate the achievement. Treat yourself to something you enjoy, take time for yourself.

8. *Evaluate your business and marketing strategies*, and if they aren't working, don't be afraid to try something else. Keep trying until you come across what works best for you.

9. *Exercise.* Take care of your health and when stressed, step away for a short time and come back to the situation. You may find it is not as complicated or difficult as you first thought.

10. *Become known among your peers*; be willing to share and you will receive more than you give.

11. *Network on and offline*, and within your local community by engaging industry organizations, business associations, and even hobbies groups.

12. *Don't be afraid to ask for help* and a referral.

13. *Join industry associations, networks, and online forums.*

14. *Participate in industry conventions and trainings.*

More information on these conventions, trainings, and associations are available in the Appendix.

Are You on a Mission?

At any given moment, most business support service owners have a very clear understanding of the mission of their company. It may not be written down, but they know what they are doing, how and where it's being done, and who their customers are. Most of the operators we talked with didn't have a formal written mission statement, but they could clearly and concisely articulate their mission when asked (see the Mission Statement Worksheet on page 28).

Stat Fact
In a survey of business owners, 68 percent have a mission statement.

If you're a solo operator and want to stay small, it's probably enough for you to keep your mission statement in your head. But if you have employees and want to eventually become a large company, it will help if you are guided by a written mission statement that can be easily communicated to others.

"A mission statement defines what an organization is, why it exists, its reason for being," says Gerald Graham, dean of the W. Frank Barton School of Business at Wichita State University in Kansas. "Writing it down and communicating it to others creates a sense of commonality and a more coherent approach to what you're trying to do."

According to Graham, at a minimum your mission statement should define who your primary customers are, identify the products and services you produce, and describe the geographical location in which you operate. For example, your mission statement might read, "Our mission is to provide small and midsize businesses in the Atlanta area with quality administrative support, including word processing, desktop publishing, and other computer-related services, done accurately and delivered on time at a reasonable price."

A mission statement should be short—usually just one sentence and certainly no more than two. A good idea is to cap it at 100 words. Graham says it is more important to adequately communicate the mission statement to employees than to customers. "Sometimes an organization will try to use a mission statement primarily for promotion and then, as an aside, use it to help the employees identify what business they're in," he says. "That doesn't work very well. The most effective mission statements are developed strictly for internal communication and discussion, and then if something promotional comes out of it, fine." In other words, your mission statement doesn't have to be clever or catchy—just accurate.

And although your mission statement may never win an advertising or creativity award, it can still be a very effective customer relations tool. One idea is to print your mission statement on a poster-sized panel, have every employee sign it, and hang it in a prominent place so customers can see it. You can even include it on your brochures and invoices.

Sample Mission Statements

Here are a few sample mission statements that a few of our surveyed entrepreneurs submitted:

Virtual Assistant Diva Administrative Services

"Virtual Assistant Diva Administrative Services was created to assist Solopreneurs in fulfilling their business goals via exceptional Executive Assistance. Our clients' growth is our growth."

Bookkeeping and Secretarial Services

"Bookkeeping & Secretarial Services offers confidential personalized service to meet individual and business needs. We specialize in assisting individual and small business contractors. It's our commitment to provide the highest level of quality service to our clients. We listen to your concerns, ask the right questions and take the time to understand your goals and objectives. We have a broad base of knowledge and solutions that will ensure your specific needs are met."

The Times They Are a Changin'

As you work through the start-up process, you'll hear over and over about the importance of planning. And planning is indeed critical—you need to think ahead about what could happen and how you'll deal with it. But one of the most crucial aspects of planning is flexibility—no matter how thoroughly and carefully you plan, things will change.

One of the most obvious changes you'll deal with almost daily is technological advances. That will have an impact on your equipment and software, the services you provide, and your relationship with your clients. It's important that you pay attention to changes in technology that will affect both you and your clients.

You'll probably also see an evolution in your service package and client base. It may be because of technology, but it may also be because the market changes or your own preferences change. For example, Joann Voss founded her business targeting the legal market and court reporters. Today, she does very little legal work; instead, her business is divided into two primary market groups: the insurance industry and audio and video production companies. Joann made the change because she found these markets more lucrative and more interesting than the legal market. She says it's easier to get people to work for you if you have fascinating work for them to do. This illustrates the wisdom of not getting so locked into your original plan that you fail to recognize opportunities when they appear.

Mission Statement Worksheet

To develop an effective mission statement, ask yourself these questions:

○ Who are my clients? _____

_____

○ Why does my company exist? Who do we serve? What is our purpose?

_____

_____

_____

○ What are our strengths, weaknesses, opportunities, and threats?

_____

_____

○ Considering the above, along with our expertise and resources, what business should we be in?

_____

_____

_____

○ What is important to us? What do we stand for?

_____

_____

_____

Now that you've answered those questions, you are ready to write your own mission statement. Use the area below.

_____

_____

_____

_____

_____

_____

Executive Stress Office Support

"Executive Stress Office Support provides clients with high quality, confidential Executive VA services in an efficient, timely and cost-effective manner."

Go2REassistant

"To provide expert support to Realtors enabling them to effectively utilize their time, money and give them a competitive edge. To ensure that Realtors have the right tools and resources to meet and exceed the expectations of their clients."

Build Your Plan

So now you need to plan how you want to start your business.

The Start-Up Planning Checklist below is one to hang onto while we explore how you start your own business support service. This is not everything you need to know, but it's always helpful to have a basic checklist to use along the way.

Start-Up Planning Checklist

Background Planning

❑ assess your strengths and weaknesses

❑ establish your personal and professional goals

❑ assess your financial resources

❑ identify the financial risks

❑ determine the start-up costs

❑ decide on your work location—home or office?

❑ do your target market research

❑ identify your customers

❑ identify your competitors

❑ develop a business plan

❑ develop a marketing plan

Start-Up Planning Checklist, continued

Business Transactions

❏ select a lawyer

❏ choose a business structure (sole proprietorship, partnership, corporation, etc.)

❏ create your business (register your business name, incorporate, etc.)

❏ select an accountant

❏ select a banker

❏ set up a business checking account

❏ apply for business loans (optional)

❏ establish a line of credit

❏ select an insurance agent

❏ obtain business insurance

First Steps of Implementation

❏ get business cards

❏ review local business codes

❏ get your furniture, equipment, and software

❏ get a federal employer identification number (if you have employees)

❏ get a state employer identification number (if you have employees)

❏ send for federal and state tax forms

❏ join professional organizations and associations

❏ set a business opening date!

Whether your goal is a part-time homebased business to supplement the family income or a full-time commercial company with employees and tremendous income and growth potential, you need to start with a written business plan. This helps you think through what you're doing, see your strengths and weaknesses, and figure out a way to overcome challenges on paper before you actually have to face them in real life. Writing a business plan is a necessary chore; it's creating the foundation and setting the vision of your company. It won't make you an automatic success but it will bypass

Stat Fact

Of the 40 surveyed entrepreneurs, 65 percent had written a business plan and many remarked that it gave them a guide to what they wanted to achieve in the next few years even if they weren't looking for financing. Most of the remaining 35 percent had mentioned that it would have probably prevented some mistakes later on.

some common causes of business failure, such as unanticipated expenses or an inadequate marketing plan.

Business Plan Basics

What is a business plan? A business plan explains your business goals, your strategies you'll use to meet them, the amount of money needed to start and keep going until you're profitable, and addresses any foreseeable problems. There are three basic sections to a business plan: the business concept, the marketplace, and the finances. If we look into these three sections further, you will find seven major components, not to mention a cover, title page, and table of contents:

1. Executive summary
2. Business description
3. Market strategies
4. Competitive analysis
5. Design and development plan
6. Operations and management plan
7. Financial factors

Executive Summary

The executive summary should be written last because it basically sums up everything in the business plan as a condensed version of what's inside. Make sure you have completed everything else and then come back to the executive summary when you know what your main points are. When you do write it, it will tell the reader about the business, its business structure (sole proprietor, LLC, etc), the amount of money needed to launch, the repayment schedule if you are using a loan, what you would do with the loan and the equity balance after the loan, which is all much simpler if you are not looking for outside funding. The simpler the money situation, the eas-

Smart Tip

According to the Small Business Administration, there are four basics for small business success: sound management practices, industry experience, technical support, and planning ability. Check it out online at www.sba.gov.

Tip...

ier the business plan will be. Remember that the executive summary should only be a page or less and make sure it sounds professional.

Business Description

Your business description is a great exercise for you since you are putting down all of your research that you've done in your planning stage in a report. In this section, start with a description of the industry and its size. Explain why it's growing and what industry trends are causing that growth. Pull out statistics and industry information about why starting a business in this industry is a great opportunity. Go on to explain your target market and your marketing strategies and then describe the services you will offer, which we will cover in Chapter 6. Explain why your portfolio of business support services will make you competitive in the marketplace and set you apart from your competitors. If you are looking for funding, explain why the funds will make your business more profitable and what you will use it for.

Market Strategies

Your market strategies section will be one of the factors that may best help you in this industry since many of our contributing business support owners said not focusing on this area was one of their biggest mistakes.

Describe your market—its size, structure, growth potential, trends, and sales (projects) potential. Use your research to focus on your future customers and the existing competition. How much of the current market will your business be able to capture? Do your best on this section since many of your future customers may not even know the advantages of outsourcing business support services. This may be a section to come back to once we further investigate your target market in Chapter 5. However, this section is important to determining how you will develop your pricing strategies. Be sure to emphasize your unique selling proposition (USP) which we will bring up throughout this book, which simply means "what makes you different?" Once you have defined your market, you need to explain your pricing strategy and distribution method.

Your pricing strategy will probably change once you get into the business, but you should project your costs now, then determine your pricing based on the profit percentage you think you can achieve. Calculate your costs such as materials, advertising, any overhead costs, and make sure to overestimate since it's always better to give yourself some wiggle room.

Your distribution method will be up to you—are you going to deliver your projects to your

> "My biggest mistake was poor marketing strategies when I first started."
>
> —Michelle Schoen,
> The Permanent Record

customers' doors or are they going to come to you? We will address shipping methods in Chapter 11, but keep it in mind when you are planning.

Competitive Analysis

Now check out the competition around you. Most business support service owners worked with small businesses in their area so they didn't concern themselves with competitors in another state or hours away. How will your business relate to the services offered by similar businesses close to you? Are there any? If there are, how are you different? Lay out the strengths and weaknesses of each one and pinpoint the strategies that will set you apart and emphasize how you can capitalize on those weaknesses. Since this industry is so diverse, it's easy to believe that there aren't others out there conducting a business like the one you're planning, but every business has competition, whether it's direct or indirect. If you do your competitive analysis properly, you will prove that you have identified your competition and have come up with a plan to deal with them.

Design and Development Plan

If you have an idea of the services you want to provide, plan to improve your current services, or want to introduce a new service, this section is especially important. You need to cover the market development and organizational development of this service. Outline the costs of adding this service, how you will market it, add it to your organizational package, and create a schedule of profitability.

Operations and Management Plan

This section is for you to explain how you will run your business and who is involved. This section will be pretty short if you are the only one running the business, but even so, use this as a marketing section for you. Explain your role in the business and list your qualifications and what you will be managing.

Financial Factors

The financial statements are the backbone of your business plan and help keep the expense surprises to a minimum. This is your forecast in the short and long term and helps estimate how long until you are profitable.

You will need to draft an income statement, cash flow statement, and balance sheet. The income statement details your cash-generating

Smart Tip

Need more help? The Small Business Administration (SBA) has online tutorials and sample plans for you to check out. Go to www.sbaonline.sba.gov/ starting/indexbusplans.html.

Tip...

Stat Fact

Of our 40 surveyed entrepreneurs, 50 percent were profitable with their business support services within 3 to 12 months. Fifteen percent were profitable immediately.

ability using revenue, expenses, depreciating capital, and cost of goods. Create a monthly income statement for your first year, then quarterly statements for the second year, and then annual statements for the following years. Most businesses draft a five-year projection. The cash-flow statement tracks the money coming and going out of your business in the same format as income statements (monthly, quarterly, then annually). This report will give you a profit or loss at the end of each term and then carry it over into the next report to show a cumulative amount. Watch this closely because if you see that you are cumulatively operating at a loss, it shows that you will need more capital than you first anticipated. Your balance sheet shows your venture's financial strength in terms of assets, liabilities, and equity. You only need to create one for each year, not monthly. If there is any other important financial information not explained anywhere else in your business plan, such as your break-even point make sure to note it here. This section may seem the hardest to you but enlist the help of an accountant if you get stuck. It's important to give yourself a financial roadmap for your business and it will help avoid money mishaps.

Long-Term Planning

Beyond starting up and managing the day-to-day operations of your company, you need to think about the future. Even if all you want is to be a small, one-person shop, you need to have a plan to maintain your workload, income level, and client base.

"Even when I have all the work I want, I take the time to network," says entrepreneur Charlene Davis. "My business may be small, but it's a long-term commitment, and I want to protect it. And even though I don't need to make a lot of money, I want to be able to forecast my revenue with some degree of accuracy, and that takes thought and planning."

The point is, no matter how busy you get in the present, you always need to have one eye on the future to assure the continuing success of your operation. Pull out your business plan every year and take another look at it. What has changed? What are your new goals? How has your business done in the past year compared to your projections? You should always be planning and working on improving your business, and keeping an up-to-date business plan means that you know what it takes to make it profitable. Now let's look at some business support services you can offer your clients.

Business
Support Services

It used to be that the majority of the work for business support services was word processing, and many businesses could survive offering that alone. But times have definitely changed, and even though there might be word-processing work out there, you need to diversify into other specialty areas.

Entrepreneur Bill Pypes agrees that while word processing is a good core service, it's vital for the new business owner to diversify into at least two other higher-end specialties, such as desktop publishing, web design, internet research, event planning, etc. He agrees that a new business owner can't make it with word processing alone. "There will always be something that's a little more complicated to do," he says. "You have to find new markets."

So what services should you offer? That's a decision you'll make based on your own individual skills, your personal preferences, and your goals for your company. If you're planning to stay small and do most of the work yourself, you'll want to specialize in services you enjoy and do well. If you plan to assemble a team of workers with a variety of skills, you can offer a much broader scope of services. Here's what a few of the business owners we talked with offer:

- *Charlene Davis* primarily does word processing and desktop publishing. She produces an association newsletter and manages that client's membership database, and also does tape transcription and other administrative support work for her clients.
- *Bill Pypes* says the majority of his business is resumes, but he also does a substantial amount of transcription, along with word processing dissertations for graduate students and some work for small businesses and independent sales representatives who work out of their homes.
- *Joann Voss* targets two primary markets: insurance and television production. For the insurance market, she transcribes recorded statements by people who have been involved in car accidents. Her other main market is television production companies that need audiotape and videotape transcription.

You can offer a wide range of services or bundle services together to offer a complete service package. The following list encompasses what we found on the market, but it is by no means exhaustive. A business support service could be almost anything, so do a self analysis to see how your background and training can develop your service portfolio.

Service Descriptions

Some of these services could be businesses in and of themselves; others are ancillary to a primary service. Listen to your clients; they'll let you know what they need, and then you can decide if you can provide it.

1-800 Telephone Call Center Service

A 1-800 telephone call center service is an answering service that caters to companies that sell products via mail order, classified advertising, and infomercials. This service can be operated from a home office and clients can call-forward their toll-free lines to your office for after-hours inquiry. You can charge a monthly fee for this service or charge by phone call received. You will need specialized and costly telephone equipment to handle the heavy call volume.

Answering/Voicemail Service

This is a great service opportunity for a homebased business since most small-to-midsized businesses pride themselves on being more personal than the larger companies in the industry, and they want to make sure that there is always a friendly voice when a customer calls even if it's after normal business hours. Therefore, many small businesses need a personalized answering service that sounds like a knowledgeable administrative assistant. Customers for this type of service include small businesses and/or individuals like plumbers, contractors, and repairmen, who often miss opportunities by not returning a call or not being available immediately. This is a great add-on service if you are already offering other services. The fees you can charge for this service will depend on your location and your customer base, but many small businesses will pay for a high-quality answering service if you can prove that you helped them earn a couple extra customers!

Consult with your telephone company for information on the necessary equipment and setup costs.

Association Management Service

This type of service is also commonly known as Executive Director Services and it provides management support to organizations, associations, and clubs that have grown beyond being run just by volunteers. Services include membership management, dues collection, accounting, marketing and advertising, and possibly some writing such as publishing the monthly newsletter. Granted, the more services you can offer each association, the more you can charge per hour. The more efficient you are at these tasks, the more customers you can handle. Getting into this service requires extensive networking and a great place to start is getting involved with organizations where you're already a member.

Billing and Invoice Service

Billing is a time-consuming task that takes up a lot of billable time for small businesses and independent professionals, and many would rather be spending their time on their businesses instead of mailing out invoices. If you are already offering other accounting-type services, this might be a great add-on service to a few of your customers. You could offer to schedule a regular pickup of your client's transaction

▲

reports and keep track of the payments, update the client's customers' accounts, and send out current invoices with any number of currently available accounting software programs. Another add-on would be to offer collections services to these clients if they have any late-paying accounts.

Bookkeeping Service

Similar to offering a billing and invoicing service, bookkeeping is another mandatory task for all small businesses. Taxes and financial laws make bookkeeping more complex every year so many entrepreneurs outsource this work to professionals who keep up with the changes. Bookkeeping services include tasks like keeping financial records, reconciling bank statements, doing payroll, preparing financial reports, and tax preparation. If you don't have a background in accounting or aren't looking to get certified, this is probably not the service for you. However, if you are financially-minded, there is a lot of business for this service and through networking; you may even get some referral business from local CPA firms.

Business Plan Writing Service

The job of a business plan writer entails laying out the plan for the small business or developing a plan for an established business to show growth strategies if they are looking to get funds for expansion. This service is for business support entrepreneurs who have business plan experience and can customize a plan to show the projections of expenses and feasibility. There is software out there already to create business plans but many clients don't want a standard plan and instead would like an expert to help them, especially if they are looking to franchise or be acquired.

Collection Service

This service is always going to be in demand since small businesses are always struggling with delinquent accounts, and large collection agencies often don't look to serve smaller companies with smaller balances. This service requires great people skills since you will be working directly with the people who owe your client money. Check with your state laws on this one and make sure that you get all of your required licenses to practice this service. If you get enough clients, this could be a very lucrative business support service.

College Paper/Report Preparation

Students at both the undergraduate and graduate levels often turn to professionals to type and format their theses, dissertations, and other important projects. Universities can be extremely particular in how these documents are formatted, and many students don't have the time or inclination to figure out how to do it right, so they're willing to pay someone to do it for them. The schools publish instructions and often even sell a software template with the correct formatting; contact the university for details on how to get this information. Some students may ask you to edit their papers; WordCares' Bill Pypes says he does this only when the student has the professor's permission.

Computer Training Service

Offering computer training services can be a great complement to other business support services you could be offering your clients. If you are already an expert on a certain software program, you may want to offer your clients workshops to train their current employees to be more efficient or contact local companies to lead corporate training classes. You will also need to have good training and presentation skills to make this service a success. It could be a great supplement to your current service offerings.

Copywriting Service

Businesses often use written materials to sell their products or services such as printed brochures or direct mail sales letters, and developing the well-written content can sometimes be difficult. Copywriters prepare the text and sometimes the design for ads, brochures, instructional manuals, media kits, catalogs, annual reports, speeches, and any other written materials that would be shown to their customers, and it takes skill and talent to capture the attention of readers and motivate them to use your clients' product or service. If you are already looking to offer desktop publishing and word processing services, this is a great extension to those services. Be sure to start a portfolio of your past works with other clients to show your expertise.

Consulting Service

This covers a wide range of issues and will depend on your particular areas of expertise. For example, you may be able to work with a client in getting his or her own office set up, equipped, and properly staffed. When you work with a client in a problem-solving or advisory capacity, you should be paid for your time as a consultant. Make sure that you have a firm background in the area that you are consulting on and provide references of small businesses to whom you've offered similar services. For more on this topic, see Entrepreneur's *Start Your Own Consulting Service*.

Desktop Publishing Service

All businesses have the need for desktop publishing services, and many small businesses would rather outsource the work instead of hiring a full-time designer to work inhouse on annual reports, brochures, catalogs, charts, graphics, fliers, ads, proposals, business cards, newsletters, printed materials, and more. This service requires advanced computer software skills to offer typesetting, document formatting and conversion, graphic and image placement and manipulation, font and text design, and an eye for design. If you are artistically-inclined and can learn the design programs, this can be a very lucrative service to offer your clients. For more on this service, check out Entrepreneur's *Start Your Own Desktop Publishing Business*.

> **Tip...**
>
> **Smart Tip**
>
> Limit the number of no-charge revisions you'll do on a desktop-publishing project. Certainly you won't charge for correcting any mistakes you may have made that the client catches, but if the client keeps making design changes after approving the initial plan, you should be compensated for your time.

Electronic Clipping Service

This service also known as an Alert Service helps businesses and professionals stay up-to-date on important industry information in newspapers, journals, magazines, blogs, web sites, and other media. Your job is to find any pertinent information that could be useful to your client, clip it, and either send the original version of the article or send them abstracts of the content, depending on what your client prefers. Clipping services usually charge a monthly fee depending on how much time you spend online. For more information on this service, check out Entrepreneur's *Start Your Own Information Consultant Business*.

Event and Meeting Planning Service

The industry for this service has gotten very competitive, but if you can get your foot in the door and show that you are thorough and detail-oriented, this could be a great business support service for you. Businesses often need support in arranging trade shows, sales conferences, product announcements, seminars, training workshops, and company parties. Meeting and party planning is a business field of its own, but you may be able to help your clients with small events and meetings, particularly if your office has conference space available. To get a complete guide to this service, check out Entrepreneur's *Start Your Own Event Planning Business*.

Home Office Planning Service

This underestimated service is from Entrepreneur's *Ultimate Start-Up Directory* and you may even need a specialist of this service when starting your own home-based business. A home office planner helps with the transition of turning a functional room into a home office and works closely with the client to develop successful work and organization plans and programs tailored to their needs and goals. They can also help with office layout design, storage solutions, work routine schedules, computer and telephone integration, and suitable equipment requirements. This is also a viable service to market to corporations since many companies are transitioning to telecommuting.

Legal Transcript/Deposition Digesting

Lawyers often need assistance in summarizing documents that explain necessary background information for their cases, and it can make for a lucrative service. Depositions are testimonies taken by a court reporter and then the information is transcribed (see Legal Transcription Service) into a lengthy document that lawyers need to review before trial. Deposition digestion services identify relevant points, summarize the transcript, and then index the information for future use. Although there is a high demand for this service, you should have a legal background or take some paralegal courses before offering this service.

Legal Transcription Service

A great service to pair with deposition digestion is a legal transcription service. Most state and federal courts have court reporters transcript the court proceedings, many other kinds of legal hearings are recorded on tape to later be transcribed. You will need to have experience in this field and an excellent typing ability and transcriptionists are often paid on a per-page basis. Accuracy is imperative for this service and if you already have a legal background and are willing to invest in the training necessary, this could be a lucrative service for you.

Logo Design Service

This is an extension of desktop publishing, but it requires graphic design experience and advanced training. To show your ability, you can create logos for fictional companies to build your portfolio when you are trying to gain a book of business. It may take time to establish a client base, but referrals from those clients should keep a strong workflow.

Mailing List Service

This easy-to-enter service is can be a great add-on to the other business support services you may already be offering. You can compile and maintain the mailing list for your clients using their customer information and help make that information a great sales tool. You could also specialize in selling mailing lists that you develop or purchase from other businesses for a specific target market or industry. You shouldn't aim for name volume since there are large mailing list companies out there, but rather tailor your lists to specific areas like your local community. Another option for this service could be to develop a campaign using your client's list and lead the project from printing, sorting, addressing, and mailing yourself.

Mail Receiving and Forwarding Service

Clients without a commercial office and clients who are on the road frequently need a service that will accept their mail and packages, and either hold it for them or forward it to wherever they happen to be. You can set up a simple system for sorting and storing your clients' mail, or you can put up mailboxes like those used by the United States Postal Service (USPS). This is a low-cost add-on service that can bring in a steady profit.

Medical Billing Service

You will often see ads asking for medical claims billing assistance and one way to earn customers would be to reply to those ads and tell them about your business support service company. Given that many of the baby boomers are retiring soon, the demand for this service has increased since doctors are required to submit all claims to Medicare on behalf of their patients. You will need specialized experience to succeed in this service and extensive training to adhere to all the rules and regulations. For more information on this service, check out Entrepreneur's *Start Your Own Medical Claims Billing Service*.

Medical Transcription Service

Medical transcription, like legal transcription, deposition digesting, and medical billing, is all very specialized and should only be offered if you have specialized training as well as a background in these fields. However, since medical transcriptionists require so much expertise, they are always in demand to produce typed reports from dictations from doctors, nurses, and other medical practitioners. The training for this service can take years to learn all the technical information for each field, but then you can offer more for your services once you become specialized in a certain field. Do your homework on the necessary training for this service before you build it into your plan. For more on medical transcription services, see Entrepreneur's *Start Your Own Medical Transcription Service*.

Newsletter Publishing Service

Pick almost any interest or field and you will find a newsletter on the topic. You will need desktop publishing experience to thrive with this service and there are several different ways to make profits. You can publish your own newsletter and charge subscription fees, advertising placement, and distribution by mail, fax, or online. Another option is to develop and maintain a newsletter for a company or organization to communicate with their members on a regular basis. Some professionals would like a template newsletter sent to a regular group of customers that is customized with the client's name for advertising. This service could pair well with an association management service and a mailing list service.

Notarizing Service

This service requires you to go get your notary certification. The training only takes a day or so and a test. Once completed, you can notarize signatures for your clients and provide other notary services as your state's laws permit; this is especially helpful for commercial-based operations that might also get some walk-in clients. There should be notary certification programs in your area, so search them online. You can also check out the National Notary Association's web site at www.nationalnotary.org.

Online Advertising Consulting Service

Some estimates say that over 1,000 businesses start a web site and need to advertise their products and/or services. If you are already working with your clients for webpage development, this could be a great specialized add-on service. Once a business has built their site, they will need to do online marketing in order to get the greatest return on their investment. An online advertising consultant helps the client develop an advertising program tailored to their needs. Is a banner advertising program a good fit for your client? What other sites should be linked to theirs? How do they use ad words? All of these questions can be answered in a tailored online advertising program.

Packing and Shipping Service

You may handle packing items and shipping parcels through a variety of ground and overnight carriers, such as UPS, Airborne, Federal Express, DHL, USPS, and others. For this service, charge your client a small handling fee. Also, you may receive a discount from the carriers that you can absorb as your profit or pass along to your clients.

Payroll Preparation Service

If you have already decided that your business support services are going to be accounting-based, then this is another great service to add to your business package. Like with many other administrative tasks, small business owners often prefer to outsource so that they can focus on growing their businesses. Federal and state tax laws change so often that entrepreneurs want an expert working on their payrolls that can give their businesses personal attention. Since your clients will most likely be small-to-midsized businesses, you can probably handle a sizable book of businesses and charge less than the large payroll companies. Just make sure that you have a written agreement with your clients that you are not liable for any mistakes on the client's behalf.

Stat Fact

According to the Small Business Administration, 25 percent of businesses are dissatisfied with their current payroll method.

Phone-In Dictation

If you're going to offer transcription, you may want to set up a system where clients can dictate over the phone into a special system that stores their words either on tape or electronically. You then transcribe their dictation as you would if it had been supplied to you on tape. The industry updates their technology regularly so check out more info online.

Photocopying Service

Even though your clients may own their own photocopying machines, they may still need you to make copies for them. Also, if you're in a commercial location, you may get some walk-in traffic for copy services. Beyond basic photocopying, they may need the reports run on a higher quality printer or photocopier or may need collation services done. If you know that your client will need to make a large photocopying run, offer to do it for them so that the deliverable to them is the end product, which is giving them more than what they expected. Or, to make them aware of your service, offer to complete photocopying project for them for free to show that you can prepare complete packets.

Print Brokering Service

Some of the work you'll do for clients will be sent to a printer for volume reproduction. You can help out your clients and add to your own revenue by functioning as a broker on the printing; you do the shopping and get the best price, quality, and service package, and then supervise the project for your client. You'll earn a commission from the printer for your efforts.

Proofreading Service

If you are offering other product development services like copywriting and resume preparation, this is a great service to add-on. This service can involve comparing a new document against an original to be sure they are the same, or reading a document and checking for spelling, grammar, and punctuation mistakes. Make sure you have a firm understanding of style manual formats and have a keen eye for details. Your service won't be worth much if the work still comes back to the client with type-os.

Public Relations Service

Public relations is the service of generating a respected profile of your business for the public and customers through press releases, press kits, speeches, brochures, television exposure, and radio time. This service is one where you should pick a niche or specialty since you need to be an expert in industry trends and perceptions. This service also has a personality requirement; you need to be outgoing, personable, and have great writing skills. Like other specialized services, this one also requires a background in communications or public relations before striking out on your own.

Resume Writing Service

Although there are programs and templates available to create resumes, it oftentimes doesn't compare to a tailored resume perused by an expert eye. Job seekers want their resumes to stand out in a pile instead of having their personal information look exactly like the next resume that they are competing against. Resumes are more than just the image; the content needs to be accurate and motivating to showcase strengths and talents. Your service in this area can range from simply typing and formatting the information provided by the client to working closely with the client to develop the content of the resume. Some people believe the latter falls more in the area of career counseling, which you may also want to do. You can expand this service by also offering cover letter services, custom letterhead, and mailing services.

Spreadsheet Design

Basic skills with spreadsheet programs are common, and if your comfort level is on par with most employees, you probably won't land much or any business. However, advanced spreadsheet design skills can make you very marketable. For example, there are dozens of advanced formula capabilities in spreadsheet programs that can be set up as a template for a small business so that they can replicate it for future use. Inputting basic data with simple formulas might not attract many customers, but offering advanced techniques is definitely a service worth selling. You may want to offer training workshops for this service as well.

Staffing Services

According to the American Staffing Association, there are numerous kinds of staffing services, and they offer great resources to business support services that wish to offer them. For more information on starting a staffing service, check out Entrepreneur's *Start Your Own Staffing Service*. Below, the American Staffing Association briefly describes the differences between each service type:

- *Long-term and contract help.* This form of service is when a staffing firm supplies eligible employees to work on long-term, indefinite assignments and projects. These employees are recruited, screened, and assigned by the staffing firm for each client's needs.

- *Managed services.* This service is more hands-on for the staffing company since they assume full responsibility for the employee as they perform a specific customer function for the client, such as working in the mail room on an on-going basis.

- *Payrolling services.* This form of service involves the client recruiting the employees but then asking the staffing company to hire them and assign them to perform the services. Another version of this service is if the employees are already working for the client, but then they are placed on the payroll of the staffing firm. Payrolling is different than a Professional Employment Organization (PEO) because the workers are usually on temporary assignments and make up a small proportion of the client's work force.

- *Placement services.* This staffing service is when a staffing company brings together eligible candidates and potential employers for the purpose of establishing a permanent employment relationship. The staffing company is usually hired by the employer when seeking a select group of eligible candidates for a specific position. For more information on this form of service, check out Entrepreneur's *Start Your Own Executive Recruiting Service*.

- *Temporary help services.* Temporary help services consist of an employment company hiring its own employees and assigning them to support or supplement a client's work force in situations involving employee absences, temporary skill shortages, seasonal workloads, and special projects.

- *Temporary-to-hire.* A temp-to-hire service is when a staffing company pairs an employee with a client to work during a trial period on a temporary basis during which both assess a "fit" and then will consider a permanent employment arrangement where the temporary employee may get hired by the client. If it is not a good match, then the service acts like a temporary help arrangement, and the employee remains employed by the staffing company.

Tape Transcription

Businesses and individuals frequently need a hardcopy transcript of material on audiotape or videotape. It could be a speech, lecture, interview, or radio or television show. You may also have clients who provide you with taped dictation, and you transcribe the material and follow the instructions they give you. As we discussed earlier, legal and medical transcription are two specialty areas that require familiarity with the professions, terminology, and formatting requirements.

Tax Preparation Service

This service requires an accounting background and possibly additional training and certification courses. This service is for complicated tax preparation needs, not basic forms that can be completed with off-the-shelf tax preparation software. Your small business clients may be giving you bookkeeping business, and when they get to the end of the year, you probably know their books better than they do, and they may naturally look to you to file their end-of-the-year paperwork. To keep your marketing targeted, you will probably be best off marketing to business instead of individuals personal income tax needs.

Telemarketing Service

Companies are always looking for professional telemarketers simply because they get results and clients rarely hesitate to pay top rates to secure a telemarketing service to promote or sell their products or services. If you have been a successful telemarketer in the past, this may be an additional service for you, but it's not for everyone.

Web Site Design and Maintenance

This service requires advanced design skills to design web sites and handle updates and changes for your clients. You can design completely customized sites for your clients or purchase basic templates and modify them for your clients' needs. You can also offer the following included services: domain name, web hosting, content updates, e-mail address support, search engine optimization, search engine submission, and more. Once you have developed a portfolio of professional web sites, use them as examples for your future clients.

Word Processing

This is a service that should be a component of other services you may provide. Essentially, it's the task of creating typed documents, manipulating them according to your clients' needs, and then modifying them into various formats. Basic word processing isn't going to give you a competitive edge, but coupling it with expert skills like understanding large document shortcuts will save you and your clients time. Word processing is the one service that all business support services have in common. Even if you think you know everything you need to know about word processing, take a quick expert course on the software programs to see if there are any new capabilities you could learn.

While these are just a few services you can offer, it's a good example of how many business support services are available and how you can pair up multiple services to give yourself a tailored service package to offer your clients. Maybe it helped you get ideas on how to expand.

Expanding Your Service Offerings

If you have already decided on a service area, here are some specific services by type that you can explore to expand your opportunities. According to the Alliance for Virtual Businesses, a business support owner, "can expand their market share by first identifying their specialty and niche, qualifying their ideal client and then listening as they describe their "wants." The owner should develop specialist skills associated with client needs and market those services as benefits for increased business growth and profitability. They will eventually become recognized as an expert in their chosen specialty, which they can then build upon to develop a new specialty, niche, and service offering."

Below are business categories with specific services to help you brainstorm on how you can expand your specialty:

Office Support Services

- Manage mailing lists
- Records management service
- Project management service
- Traveling notary service
- Temporary office help
- Proofreading and editing services
- Home office organization services
- Office organization services
- Professional event planning services

Transcription Services

- Interview transcription service
- Medical transcription service
- Focus group transcription service
- Round table discussion transcription service
- Legal transcription service
- Audio tape enhancement service
- Audio file conversion service
- Video transcription service
- CD transcription service

Business Document and Design Support Services

- Desktop publishing services
- Graphic design service
- Conference recording services
- Webcast teleconferencing services
- Foreign language translation services
- Technical writing services
- APA formatting and editing services
- CD cover and booklet design and printing services
- Graphic illustration service
- PowerPoint presentation design service

Accounting Services

- Bookkeeping services
- Bookkeeping prep work service

Tax Preparation and Filing Services

- Quickbooks or Quicken support
- Peachtree support

Computer and Software Training Services

- Web site design workshop

- ACT! training service
- Advanced Excel training
- Advanced PowerPoint training
- HTML, DHTML, JavaScript, and PHP programming workshops
- MySQL database training service
- Flash, FrontPage, Pagemaker, and Dreamweaver training

Web Site Design Services

- Web site design and development service
- Web site hosting service
- Contact form data collection support
- Web site backend development support
- Business development solutions

Flash Presentations and Dynamic Graphics Service

- Search engine optimization and Google page ranking support

Sales and Marketing Support Services

- Branding expertise
- New product launch support
- Corporate branding initiatives
- Lead conversion support
- Drip e-mail marketing campaigns
- CRM (customer relationship management) support
- Public relations support
- Online promotions consulting
- Special events marketing and management services

Training for Success

After looking at all of your service options, it's important to note that there is experience and training required for most of them. Assess your current skill set and background and see which services appeal most to you. Maybe there are some services that you would like to offer your clients, but you don't feel confident in your expertise. Budget training classes into your plan since you are your business and investing in yourself is investing in your business's success! Check out classes at your local community college or contact the organizations and associations in the Appendix and ask about training courses or certification programs.

Sharon Williams of the Alliance for Virtual Businesses says that the following software training is important for your business support service even though your needs are going to vary depending on which services you offer and your niche.

- Microsoft software since they are bundled with most PCs, such as Excel, Powerpoint, Word, Photo Editor, etc.
- Ability to record and edit MP3 files for uploading to client web sites
- Autoresponder (see definition in Glossary)
- Blog management
- Basic web creation, maintenance, and search engine optimization
- Niche specialty software such as real estate marketing, transaction coordination, calendar management

Other business support service owners said that they took several online courses and tutorials to freshen their skills. The key is to keep investing in your abilities so that you're abreast of the industry changes.

We asked Lyn Prowse-Bishop what training she did to prepare or to expand her services. She said that, "I've taken a training course in InDesign software as one of my clients wanted me to use it for his newsletters. I will shortly be undertaking a medical terminology course to better enable me to service my doctor clients. I'm also preparing to teach myself (or undertake a more formal online course) in Dreamweaver so that I can expand into web site maintenance, not design, just maintenance. I would like to do an intermediate course in Access, and I've just purchased ACT! for another client and will need to learn how to use this program as well. All these changes come from existing client requests but will obviously enable me to expand my services into other areas once my skills become proficient enough." She went on to say that, "I think that someone starting a business in this industry needs to have at least an intermediate skill level in the software they will be using, such as Microsoft Office programs. I also think that they should have past experience in their specialty. For example, if you are offering bookkeeping services, they should have worked previously as a bookkeeper or in the finance department of an organization. They might benefit too from attending some online seminars on

"Before you can answer the question of 'What training should someone starting a business in this industry do?' you have to know who your target market is going to be. If you're going to be working with medical professionals, you need to be up-to-date on the latest medical terminology. If you're going to work with real estate professionals, you need to have good marketing and sales skills."

—Michelle Schoen,
The Permanent Record

▲

how to network effectively because it's very important to be able to network to gain more business."

Diana Ennen said that "I already had medical terminology experience, so that was helpful. Later in my business I went back and got my paralegal degree to help with my legal transcription. That was extremely beneficial as then I understood more what I was typing and why I was typing it. Today, I'm always attending seminars and tele-classes."

Each owner has their own niche and specialty, but each has had either the background or the training to offer their services and have continued to expand them with additional courses. Now let's take a look at targeting your market so you can choose which services are best for them.

Defining Your
Target Market

For any business to succeed it must have customers—people or companies that buy the products or services it offers. Once you've decided what services you want to offer, you need to figure out who will likely buy them, and you do that with market research. It would be impossible to develop marketing strategies without market research. This process provides you with data that will help you identify and reach particular market segments, and to solve or avoid marketing problems. A thorough market survey forms the foundation of any successful business.

The goal of market research is to identify your market, find out where it is, and develop a strategy to communicate with prospective customers in a way that will convince them to buy from you. The Market Niche Worksheet on page 57 will help you define your own market niche. You have three broad markets for your business support service: the general public, small commercial and homebased businesses, and large corporations.

General Public

By "general public," we mean individual clients who are not businesses. The two largest segments of this market are people needing resume preparation and college students.

A job hunter creating or updating a resume may actually write the document and bring it to you for layout and printing; he or she may need you to assist in writing the content as well. Even when the unemployment rate is low, the resume market is significant because people don't have to be unemployed to need a resume.

Of course, many people have their own computers and can prepare their own resumes, but they may also realize the importance of having a professionally designed document, along with a well-written cover letter, for their job search.

There are thousands of higher-learning institutions in the United States with a collective enrollment of millions of students. Although many students prepare reports and papers themselves, enough of them will turn to a professional word-processing firm to make this market substantial.

Students working on particularly long papers, such as graduate theses or dissertations, are strong candidates for your service. And, of course, once they graduate, they may come back to you for assistance with their resumes.

In addition to students, the academic community may also be a source of business (think professors who need word processing, editing, and proofreading services for their books and articles).

If you are in a commercial location and want to offer photocopying, faxing, and shipping, you may also serve the general public with these services.

Bright Idea

If you are homebased with small children, consider looking for clients that are likely to be more family-friendly, such as schools and churches. Those types of clients always seem to be more understanding of such things as bringing children along to pick up or deliver work than clients in other industries.

Market Niche Worksheet

How well have you defined your market niche? How comfortably and clearly you answer the following questions will tell you.

O Who are my clients? _____

_____

_____

O What services do they need? _____

_____

_____

O Where are they located? _____

_____

_____

O How many hours each month will I be able to bill? _____

_____

_____

O What can I expect to earn per billable hour? _____

_____

_____

O How will I communicate with my prospective clients? _____

_____

_____

_____

O Will this market niche generate sufficient revenue for me to reach my income and profitability goals? _____

_____

_____

_____

Small Businesses

Chances are, the majority of your clients will fall into this category. These are companies that may require secretarial and administrative support but do not have the money, space, or need for a full-time employee. Or they may prefer to outsource specific tasks rather than invest in the talent and equipment necessary to get the job done right. And hiring temporary employees can be more costly than small businesses' needs demand.

> "My biggest mistake was targeting everyone and anyone. Once I narrowed down my marketing efforts to small business owners, usually one-person businesses, I received more responses and more clients."
>
> —Janice Byer,
> Docu-Type Administrative and
> Web Design Services

As the number of small businesses continues to grow, so does your potential market. And the list of services they use is limited only by your imagination and personal preferences. As you develop relationships with small businesses, you'll be in a position to make suggestions that will increase the volume—or even expand the scope—of the work you do for them.

Large Corporations

Even fairly large operations with a full-time administrative staff may be candidates for your services. If a company has a temporary situation where they have more work than they can handle inhouse, they may turn to you to pick up the overload. Or, like the small businesses mentioned earlier, they may prefer to outsource special projects rather than hire temporary workers. This is a smart move, because hiring temporary employees means training them and providing them with adequately equipped workstations. Sending the work to you eliminates that hassle and cost.

Large companies also use business support services when their own staff members are unavailable due to vacations or illness. They may not actually need a "temp," that is, someone to come in and be present in the office, but they may need someone who can handle all or part of the work of the absent staffer.

Finding a Niche—or Niches

It's a good idea to select one or more key market groups to target. There are a number of valid reasons for choosing a well-defined market niche. By targeting a very specific market segment, you can tailor your service menu, marketing efforts, and customer service system to meet that segment's needs.

You can refine your marketing efforts and gain a reputation within the industry for expertise in certain areas—which means you can charge more. Think about it: In the medical field, who earns more—a family practitioner or a neurosurgeon? The neurosurgeon, naturally, because he's a specialist and what he does requires greater skill.

Some market niches you might consider include:

- *Other business support services.* Let existing business owners know you're available for overflow or to work on a contract basis. Expect to have to sign confidentiality and non-compete agreements, but be sure any such contract limits you to only being prevented from marketing directly to the service's clients whose work you actually do. You might have to discount your rates to allow them to make a profit, but your marketing and sales costs will be minimal, which offsets the discount; however, be sure you are compensated for rush jobs.

- *Specific professions or industries.* If you have expertise in a specific field, you may target your service to that field. Two of the most common are the legal and medical fields, particularly transcribing for these groups, because you'll need to be familiar with a long list of special terms and formatting requirements. Or you may want to target professional salespeople, such as manufacturers' reps, who work from their homes and need occasional administrative support.

- *Geographic areas.* If you are in a densely populated area, perhaps an office center or a light industrial park, you may want to choose your market by geography. Determine your parameters, and then market to the companies within your service area, emphasizing the convenience of using your service.

- *Academic.* If you're near a college or university, you can serve a number of academic-related niches, including students, instructors, and even administrators.

Your Potential Market: Who Needs What?

To say that there is a tremendous demand for business support services is one thing, but when it gets down to the nitty-gritty of planning your business and targeting your market, you need more specifics. Here is a short sample list of

Bright Idea
Set your rush rate at a percentage above your regular fee. For example, Joann Voss of Voss Transcriptions charges 30 percent above her regular rate for rush jobs versus some other business support services that charge 50 percent more for work clients want back in less than 24 hours.

Industry Analysis Worksheet

Use this worksheet to help you define your position in your industry and identify possible niche markets for your product.

○ Are there any new competitors in the arena? Does everyone think this is a hot idea?

_____

○ Have any gone out of business recently? Why? _____

_____

○ If there have been no new entries in the market, is it because there are fatal flaws with the concept, or because you are the first in a new idea, or because you have figured out how to overcome problems others have not solved? _____

_____

○ Are there a small number of competitors for a large market, or a large number for a small market? _____

_____

○ If all the other competitors are large companies, can you fit into a small but profitable niche, or do you have the capital to compete head-to-head, or are you at risk of being attacked by large, established corporations? _____

_____

○ If there has been no recent innovation in your market, is it because the profit margins aren't there to make it profitable, or because the corporations are getting lazy and giving you a legitimate opportunity? _____

_____

○ Is there room for improvement in the quality of service given to the market (for example, the Postal Service), which will give a new/small company an edge?

_____

○ What is the history of your market? New markets, like microwaveable foods when microwaves were first invented, grow and change quickly. Old markets, like radio manufacturing, may be more difficult to enter. In an old market you must have a new idea, a real edge. In a new market, you need to be fast. _____

_____

This worksheet was one of the free forms available at Entrepreneur.com.

typical client groups and the types of services they use:

- *Architects.* Word processing documents and proposals.
- *Associations.* Newsletters, desktop publishing, mailing lists, word processing.
- *Attorneys.* Word processing, transcription, briefs, template design, form design, articles for various publications, database design and maintenance, and newsletters.

Stat Fact

Of the 40 entrepreneurs surveyed, 48 percent have one to five regular clients that they provide support on a consistent basis. Only 22 percent support more than ten clients at a time.

- *Churches, synagogues, and religious organizations.* Newsletters, bulletins, meeting minutes, fliers, news releases, welcome packages.
- *Consultants.* Word processing, transcription, proposals, correspondence.

A Suite Market

An executive suite operation—where tenants rent office space and share common needs, such as a reception area and receptionist, copy machine, fax machine, and other equipment—can be the perfect niche for your business support service company. There are three ways to establish service in an executive suite.

1. The most common way is to actually start an executive suite company by leasing a sizable space in an office building, and then subleasing space to clients, providing them a package deal of both office space and administrative support services. Your clients' monthly rental fee would cover their office space and basic services, such as receptionist and telephone answering, and you can negotiate fees for additional services.

2. Commercial real estate developers sometimes recognize the need to provide more than just space to tenants—particularly small, growing companies. They might hire a business support service company to act as an executive suite management company, managing the property and providing office support services to the tenants.

3. You might consider entering into a joint venture agreement with a real estate developer to provide office support for tenants in a commercial building. In this sort of arrangement, your autonomy and profit potential would be greater than with the second option, but so will the degree of risk you take.

- *Copy shops*. Desktop publishing, graphic design.
- *Corporations (large)*. Manuals, transcription, special projects.
- *Graphic designers*. Text input, proofreading.
- *Individuals*. Resumes, job applications, college and graduate school applications, computer training.
- *Insurance companies, brokerages, agencies, and word processing-related businesses*. Transcription, database management, proposals.
- *Market research companies*. Focus group and interview transcription.
- *Physicians and medical offices*. Medical transcription.
- *Politicians/political campaigns*. Desktop publishing, newsletters, fliers.
- *Professors*. Transcription, articles.
- *Real estate brokers/agencies*. Database management, mailing lists, newsletters, fliers.
- *Sales representatives*. Correspondence, mailing list management, reports, newsletters, fliers.
- *Small businesses (in any industry)*. Word processing, correspondence, general administrative support, billing, newsletters, scanning, training.
- *Students*. Word-processing papers, proofreading and editing dissertations and other documents, entrance and scholarship applications, theses, transcription.
- *Writers (business, medical, technical, etc.)*. Interview transcription, research, word processing.

Understanding the Competition

One of the most basic elements of effective marketing is differentiating yourself from the competition. One marketing consultant calls it "eliminating the competition," because if you set yourself apart by doing something no one else does, then you essentially have no competition. However, before you can differentiate yourself, you first need to understand who your competitors are and why your clients might use them. See the Competitor Analysis Worksheet on page 63 to help you define your competition.

The easiest way to find your competitors is to browse through the Yellow Pages. Look under a variety of categories, including "Business

Smart Tip

Keep geography in mind as you develop your market. Though some business support services are so specialized that they have clients across the country, most serve a fairly limited geographical radius such as only a three to five mile radius from their office.

Competitor Analysis Worksheet

This worksheet will help you define your competitors. Competitors are companies that perform services similar to yours or can be substituted for the ones you plan to offer. Fill in the following table about your competitors and you may need to create additional tables to fit them all. Check out the Directory in the Appendix for some similar companies in your state.

	Competitor A	Competitor B	Competitor C
Where is your competitor located?			
What are your competitor's annual sales?			
Who are the major managers and members of the board?			
Is the company owned or in partnership with any other corporations?			
What are the competitor's strengths?			
What are their weaknesses?			
What is the company's product line?			
How do the products compare to yours, in terms of functionality, appearance, and any other criteria?			
What is their price structure?			
What are the company's marketing activities?			

Competitor Analysis Worksheet, continued

	Competitor A	Competitor B	Competitor C
What are the company's supply sources for products?			
What are the strengths and weaknesses of their sales literature?			
Is the company expanding or cutting back?			

This form is available for download at Entrepreneur.com.

Support Services," "Secretarial Services," "Desktop Publishing," "Typing Services," "Resume Services," "Notaries—Public," "Telephone Answering Services," and any other category that might cover a service you intend to offer.

For the most part, the operators we talked with have friendly relationships with their competitors. This is partly because few business support services are identical, and operators frequently turn to one another for referrals and assistance with work overloads. Call your competitors, ask to speak to the owner, and introduce yourself. Tell them you're starting a new business and you want to find out what they do so you can refer clients if you get requests for services you don't offer. You might also let them know you're available to work as a subcontractor if they need you. We've made this easy for you by creating a Directory at the end of this book of some business support service owners listed by state so you can find the competitors near you.

Bright Idea

Building owners and managers are a great source of marketing information and referrals. They know their tenants and are in a position to give you valuable information that will help you, or to even make referrals. Making these alliances is well worth the time and effort.

The easiest way to set yourself apart from the competition and build a strong, loyal client base is to offer top-notch, accurate, on-time service at reasonable rates. You don't have to be the cheapest service in town, but you do have to do quality work and deliver by your clients' deadlines.

Choosing Your
Business Location

When it comes to the actual site of your business, you have two choices: homebased or a commercial location. A business support service company can be extremely successful in either venue; your decision will depend on your individual resources and goals.

As you consider the issue of location, keep a few things in mind. Depending on the specific services you offer and market you target, you may be dealing both with the general public, who will need access to your office, and with small-business owners and managers in larger corporations who may also want to visit your facility or have their employees or a messenger pick up and deliver work.

In any business, but especially in this one, a professional image is a critical element of success. Homebased operations are very accepted in today's business world (in fact, many customers prefer dealing with homebased suppliers because they have lower overhead and can therefore charge less), but you still need to present the appearance of being a serious business, even though you may choose to work from your house. And if you opt for a commercial location, be sure it is one that is compatible with your goals.

Many operators start from home with the goal of moving into commercial space as soon as they're established with a few clients, and this is an excellent strategy. Joann Voss worked at home for the first six months and then rented office space from a friend who had a secretarial service. "I paid her $150 a month, and I also had to sit at the front desk and be her receptionist, and if she had overflow, I helped her," Joann recalls. "It was a great deal. I couldn't have started any other way because rent in the Chicago area is pretty high." Today, she's in her own large office and is subleasing space to other small businesses.

Homebased Operations

The major benefit of starting a homebased business is the fact that it significantly reduces the amount of start-up and initial operating capital you'll need. But there's more to consider than simply the upfront cash. You need to be conveniently located so your clients can get to you and/or you can get to them without wasting time traveling. Though some types of work won't require a great deal of ongoing interaction with the client, other types will. If you're doing desktop publishing, for example, your client may want to review proofs at several stages. Even if they're willing to come to you to do that, they're not going to want to drive great distances. And if they expect you to bring the proofs to them, you don't want to have to spend a lot of unprofitable time in your car.

So the first thing you need to think about is whether your home is conveniently located in relation to your target market. In addition to actual proximity, consider accessibility. If

Stat Fact
According to the Small Business Administration, experts estimate that at least 20 percent of new small businesses are homebased.

Beware!

The typical suburban home is often not the best location in which to operate a business support service company. You will most likely be isolated from commercial districts, and parking will be limited. If this is your situation, be sure your market is compatible with your location.

clients will be coming to your office, you need to be located on or near a main street. Your neighborhood may be charming, and your house perfect for a homebased business, but if your clients have to travel on a number of small side streets to reach you, they may abandon you for a more easy-to-reach provider. Along these lines, parking should be plentiful and easily available at no charge to your clients.

Next, think about your home itself. Do you have a separate room for an office, or will you have to work at the dining room table? Can you set up a comfortable workstation with all the tools and equipment you'll need? Can you separate your work area from the rest of the house so you can have privacy when you're working and get away from "the office" when you're not?

Entrepreneur.com provides numerous resources for homebased businesses and they have developed a Home Office Worksheet (page 68) to locate and design your home office space.

Even if you are able to dedicate a room to your business, keep in mind that your clients may come to your home to drop off and pick up work or to review work in progress. This means that not only does your office need to appear professional, but the other areas of your home that clients may see should be neat and orderly and reflect the impression you want to create. Leading your clients through a living room cluttered with toys or past a kitchen with dirty dishes does not create a strong professional image. Keep pets and children out of the way when clients are in your office.

Commercial Locations

If you decide on a commercial location, your range of options is fairly broad, and your choice should be guided largely by the specific services you want to provide and the market you want to reach. Starting in a commercial location requires more initial cash than starting from home, but the business you can attract by having an office location can make up for this expense.

A good location for your business is an office building with other businesses (that may also be clients) or in an executive suite (again, the other tenants may become clients). Of course, don't restrict your marketing efforts to tenants in your building; reach out to other businesses in the area.

Home Office Worksheet

List three possible locations in your home for your office, which should include a work area for you and enough space for your desk, computer, and telephone:

1. _____

2. _____

3. _____

Make a physical survey of each location:

○ Are phone and electrical outlets placed so that your equipment can easily access them? Or will you be faced with unsightly, unsafe cords snaking across the carpet?

_____

_____

○ Measure your space. Will your current desk or table (or the one you have your eye on) fit? _____

_____

○ Do you have adequate lighting? If not, can you create or import it? Is there proper ventilation? _____

_____

○ What is the noise factor? _____

_____

○ Is there room to spread out your work? _____

_____

○ Optional: How close is it to the coffeemaker? Refrigerator? (This can be either a plus or minus, depending on your current jitter factor and waistline.) _____

_____

Home Office Worksheet, continued

Next, list three possible home locations for your inventory:

1. _____

2. _____

3. _____

Again, make a survey of each location:

○ Is it climate-controlled? Will you need climate control? _____

_____

○ Is there adequate lighting, ventilation, and space for you to easily access your inventory? _____

_____

○ Will you need to construct special shelving or add other storage space? If so, make notes here: _____

_____

_____

_____

You may also want to consider a retail location, such as a shopping center. This would be appropriate if you are targeting students, individuals, and homebased business owners. It will give you some walk-in traffic for services such as photocopying and notarizing and may be more easily accessible for some of your clients than many commercial offices.

Regardless of the specific place, a commercial location gives you a degree of credibility that is hard to earn in a homebased office. You'll also have space to store the equipment and supplies you'll use in the course of your business, and create a setup that is more efficient and practical than what you might be able to do in a spare bedroom. You'll probably only need 200 to 400 square feet at first, and you should be able to find an office that size in a good location at a fairly reasonable price. Sharing office

Put Out the Welcome Mat?

A challenge for many homebased business owners is deciding where to meet with clients, particularly when they are strangers. Many business support service operators are not comfortable inviting strangers into their homes, especially if they are home alone or with small children, and this is a valid concern.

You don't need to express any fear or apprehension. Simply say "It's my policy to meet with clients either in their office or at a neutral place. Which do you prefer?"

The ideal solution is to meet at the client's office, but if this isn't practical or possible, a good alternative is to meet in a public place, such as a library, restaurant, or hotel lobby. If you must have your children with you, try a fast-food restaurant with a playground area where they can occupy themselves while you and your client discuss business.

If the client is pushy about wanting to come to your home even after you have indicated a preference for a public location, consider whether or not this is a client you would like to have. Your clients may not be a threat to your physical safety, but their disregard for your comfort level is a sign that they will probably be a difficult person to deal with.

space with a non-competing or complementary business to save money may also be an option.

In addition to the building itself, consider your location within the building. A lobby office is ideal, because it gives your clients easy access while exposing you to everyone who enters the building. A location opposite the elevator doors can also give you fairly good exposure if a number of people make stops at your floor. But an office at the end of a hallway or in a place where no one walks by will mean you have virtually no chance of attracting new business from passers-by.

Office Layout and Décor

A number of factors will influence how you arrange your office. Your layout depends on whether you are homebased or in a commercial location, and if you are a one-person shop, have employees, and so forth. Given all the variables involved, it's

Bright Idea

Consider any special market niches you plan to target when choosing your location. For example, if you intend to specialize in legal transcription, you'll want an office downtown near the courthouse, where most of the lawyers' offices are. If you plan to target students, you'll want to be near a college or university.

impossible to suggest an ideal, one-size-fits-all layout. But there are some points you need to consider.

If you're in a commercial location, it's a good idea to have a counter at the front of the office. When clients walk in, they can discuss their needs at the counter, where they can spread out any necessary documents. They can also drop off any materials you may need from them, such as letterhead, imprinted envelopes, or labels, etc. Use the counter to display your own marketing materials, policies, and other promotional items—but don't let it get too cluttered. The space under the counter can be used for storage.

If you offer photocopying or fax services, put these machines near the front counter so your clients can serve themselves where you can still keep an eye on them. Behind the counter, set up workstations for yourself and your employees.

While much of your consultation with clients can be done across a counter, if some clients need to proofread documents, you should set up a space where they can do this without distractions. Ideally, this would be a small, enclosed room, but it could also be a desk or work table off to the side of your main office. If you are offering resume writing, consulting, and career coaching, you will need an enclosed, semi-soundproofed area that allows privacy and confidentiality for your clients.

Your office décor should be businesslike, efficient, and attractive. You don't need to spend a lot of money on elegant furnishings, but you do need to make sure you create a favorable impression in your clients' minds. A good coat of paint will go a long way in brightening up your environment. Neutral shades such as beige or muted gray are good choices and will let you highlight your interior with bold graphics, posters, art prints, or bulletin boards. A few large plants will also add to the ambience, but be sure you maintain them. A

Smart Tip

Tip...

Whether you are home-based or commercial-based, be sure your office has adequate electrical capacity. You'll need an ample supply of "clean" current without fluctuations that could damage your equipment. You'll also need plenty of outlets so you can safely plug in all your equipment—many older office buildings and homes are lacking in this area. Consult with an electrician or a representative from your local power company to make sure your office has the capacity to support your needs.

healthy plant is not only attractive, but it also helps to maintain clean indoor air; a wilted, droopy plant with brown leaves may make your clients wonder just how well you'll do their work if you can't even manage to take care of a plant.

Desks and chairs should be attractive and functional but not luxurious. Invest in ergonomically sound chairs and equipment to preserve your health and productivity—and that of your employees. Be sure trash cans are emptied regularly and that the office is kept clean and dusted. Periodically take a look at your office through the eyes of a client who has never seen it before, and think about the impression it makes.

7

Choosing the
Right Equipment

Having the right equipment is a critical part of being able to provide the services your clients want and need. On the plus side, compared with many other types of businesses, your equipment needs are minimal. However, choosing the right pieces for your particular operation will take some research.

Bright Idea

Consider investing in a natural or ergonomic keyboard rather than the standard flat design. The ergonomic design is slightly curved and fits the natural positioning of the hands, which reduces hand and wrist stress and the risk of repetitive motion problems such as carpal tunnel syndrome.

Chances are, you find a trip to your local office supply superstore more exciting than a day at the mall, but resist the temptation to get carried away with exotic gadgets and "office toys." Think carefully about what you need—and don't need—do your homework, and make your buying decisions wisely.

Computers and Related Equipment

Here's a quick rundown of the basic equipment you'll most likely need.

- *Computer*. Your computer is the foundation of your business support service, and it will also help you manage bookkeeping and inventory control tasks, calculate estimates, coordinate workloads, maintain customer records, and produce marketing materials.

- *Printer*. There was a time when your choice of printers was simple: If you wanted to provide quality, you had to have a laser printer. But as inkjet technology improves and prices drop, you may be able to meet your clients' needs with a lower-priced printer. This is a judgment call you have to make, depending on the type of work you do and the quality of output you need. Points to consider include whether your clients want color output, high-density camera-ready output (for desktop-publishing projects) or if simple, good quality black-and-white printing will suffice.

- *Software*. Think of software as your computer's "brains," the instructions that tell your computer how to accomplish the functions you need. You'll need a major word-processing program, such as Microsoft Word that can read and convert files created in other formats. It's important to stay reasonably current on the version of your software; most of the upgrades are not extremely expensive, and you don't want your clients thinking your equipment is antiquated. See the worksheet on page 75 to help you determine your software needs.

Beware!

The prices on color printers are falling rapidly, and your clients may appreciate it if you have the ability to provide color output. However, the ink cartridges these printers use may drive the cost-per-page up more than you realize. If you are providing color output, be sure you've researched the cost of printing the material and set your rates accordingly.

Commonly Used Business Support Service Software

This checklist is by no means all the software programs that your clients could need you to work with so take a closer look at your software needs after finalizing your service offerings. Your software/program needs will depend on your proficiencies and services, so we've listed the software that is most commonly used by this industry:

ACT!	Microsoft Netmeeting
Adobe Acrobat	Microsoft PowerPoint
Adobe Acrobat Reader	Microsoft Project
Adobe GoLive	Microsoft Publisher
Adobe Illustrator	Microsoft Visio
Adobe InDesign	Microsoft Windows XP
Adobe PageMaker	Peachtree
Adobe Photo Deluxe	QuarkXPress
Adobe Photoshop	Quickbooks
Copernic	Quicken
CuteFTP	Skype
Eudora	Symantec Ghost
Filemaker	Symantec Internet Security
Jasc Animation Shop	Symantec Norton AntiVirus
Macromedia Dreamweaver	Symantec Norton SystemWorks
Macromedia Fireworks	Symantec Norton Utilities
Macromedia Flash	Symantec WinFax Pro
Macromedia Freehand	Time Trax
Macromedia MX	TraxTime
McAfee Personal Firewall	Trillian
Microsoft Access	WebPosition
Microsoft Excel	WinZip
Microsoft FrontPage	WS_FTP
Microsoft Money	Zone Alarm

▲

Got the Goods?

On the subject of equipment, there are a couple of issues you need to think about carefully before making the final decision on what to buy—and how to pay for it.

○ *Used or new.* Most of the operators we talked with preferred to buy new when it comes to computers, printers, and other equipment used in the delivery of their services. Though used equipment is usually a bargain from a price perspective, the technology is often out-of-date. Joann says she has had a problem with used transcription units working reliably. "I'm at the point where I will buy nothing used, especially computers, because the technology changes so rapidly," she says. The price may be much cheaper, but the reliability of used equipment is not worth the money saved. Furnishings such as desks, chairs, filing cabinets, and various office fixtures are a different story. These items can safely be purchased used at a substantial savings through dealers, classified ads, and other sources.

○ *Service contracts.* The business support service operators we spoke with didn't feel service contracts were a worthwhile investment. Charlene Davis considered and rejected the idea of a service contract on her computer, which is her primary piece of equipment. "If it falls apart, I'll just buy a new one," she says. "The technology is changing so fast that most computers are out-of-date before they begin to have problems."

○ *Lease or buy.* With computers and peripherals becoming increasingly affordable, the leasing option is becoming decreasingly viable. Most leasing companies don't want to bother with a single computer-and-printer package, and business owners find it makes more financial management sense to buy the equipment.

The software you will need depends on the services you offer. If you're going to do page layout and graphic design, you'll need a good desktop-publishing program along with some drawing and design programs. If you're going to maintain databases and mailing lists, you'll need a program designed to handle these functions; typically, they come under the "contact management software" category.

In addition to purchasing software to provide services to your clients, you'll also need programs that will handle your accounting, inventory, customer information management, and other administrative requirements. Software can be a significant investment, so do a careful analysis of your own needs and then study the market and examine a variety of products before making a final decision.

- *Scanner.* If you are going to be doing word processing from existing documents, a scanner can be a tremendous productivity tool because it can save you hours of data entry. It will also be useful if you are doing desktop publishing and presentations because it allows you to include photographs and artwork in the documents.

- *Data-backup systems.* To protect your own and your clients' electronic data, you need to routinely perform a backup. Your computer vendor can help you choose a backup system compatible with your computer.

- *Uninterruptible power supply.* To protect your computer system as well as work in progress, all of your machines should be plugged into an uninterruptible power

> ⚠️ **Beware!**
> Only work with legally purchased, properly licensed software, and be sure you read and understand the terms of your software agreement. For example, chances are your software agreement prohibits installation on multiple computers for multiple users unless you pay for that type of use. Law enforcement agencies are cracking down on software piracy; it's better to pay the price and operate legally and ethically than risk criminal charges.

supply that will provide electricity in the event of a power failure. These devices also provide a degree of protection against power surges.

One more thing you need to think about before making your final decision is whether to buy a Macintosh or a Windows-based PC. There was a time when Macs were used primarily for graphic design work and didn't have much in the way of other business software available, while Windows systems had plenty of business software but could not handle the graphics side as well as Macs. But as both systems have evolved, the differences between them have become more personal preference than capability.

Other Office Equipment

There are a few other pieces of equipment that, depending on your situation, you may need. The Business Support Service Supply Checklist and the Office Supplies Checklist on pages 80 and 81, respectively to determine these needs.

- *Typewriter.* You may think that most typewriters are in museums these days, but they actually remain quite useful to businesses that deal frequently with pre-printed and multipart forms, such as order forms and shipping documents. Most business support services will need at least one typewriter. Many business support services use them for forms, applications, and other documents that can't be completed on a computer.

- *Photocopier.* The photocopier is a fixture of the modern office and can be useful to even the smallest business support service. You can get a basic, low-end, no-frills personal copier for less than $400 in just about any office supply store. This will meet your needs if you're not doing a huge volume of photocopying for your clients. More elaborate models increase proportionately in price. If you anticipate a heavy volume, consider leasing. If you are located in a retail location, you may want to consider a coin-operated copy machine that is accessible to the public.

- *Fax machine.* Fax capability has become another essential of modern offices. You can either add a fax card to your computer or buy a stand-alone machine. If you use your computer, it must be on to send or receive faxes, and the transmission may interrupt other work. For most business support services, a stand-alone machine on a dedicated telephone line is a wise investment. Don't forget to consider the cost of toner cartridges and paper when evaluating a fax machine. These items can add up!

- *Dictation and transcription equipment.* If you are going to offer dictation or tape transcription services, you'll need the right equipment. The dictation system you buy will depend on how sophisticated you want to be and the needs of your clients. In most cases, this will not be a start-up item. Transcription machines typically handle micro, mini, and standard cassettes; which size you get will depend on the size tapes your clients use.

- *Postage scale.* Unless all of your mail is identical, and especially if you are going to be mailing materials for your clients, a postage scale is a valuable investment. An accurate scale takes the guesswork out of postage and will quickly pay for itself. It's a good idea to weigh every piece of mail when you're unsure of the weight to eliminate the risk of items being returned for insufficient postage or overpaying. Light mailers—one to 12 articles per day—will be adequately served by inexpensive mechanical postal scales, which typically range from $10 to $25. If you are averaging 12 to 24 items per day, consider a digital scale, which is somewhat more expensive—generally from $50 to $200—but significantly more accurate than a mechanical unit. If you send more than 24 items per day or use

Dollar Stretcher

A great place to shop for used furniture and equipment is the surplus office at a nearby college or university—which is where entrepreneur Bill Pypes bought his desk and a conference table he uses as a work table. If the school doesn't have a surplus office listed, call the main information number to find out which department handles disposal of used items.

priority or expedited services frequently, you may want to invest in an electronic computing scale that weighs the item and then calculates the rate via the carrier of your choice, making it easy for you to make comparisons. The availability of a high-quality postage scale can be a competitive advantage if you handle mailings for your clients.

- *Postage meter.* Postage meters allow you to pay for postage in advance and print the exact amount on the mailing piece when it is used. Many postage meters can print in increments of one-tenth of a cent, which can add up to big savings for bulk mail users. Meters also provide a "big company" professional image, are more convenient than stamps, and can save you and your clients money in a number of ways. Postage meters are leased, not sold, with rates starting at about $30 per month. They require a license that is available from your local post office. Only four manufacturers are licensed by the United States Postal Service to manufacture and lease postage meters; your local post office can provide you with contact information.

- *Paper shredder.* A response to both a growing concern for privacy and the need to recycle and conserve space in landfills, shredders are becoming increasingly common in both homes and offices. They allow you to efficiently destroy incoming unsolicited direct mail, as well as sensitive internal documents and drafts of clients' work before they are discarded. Make sure that you get a 'cross cut' shredder since the less expensive types only cut the paper lengthways.

- *Credit and debit card processing equipment.* This could range from a simple imprint machine to an online terminal. Consult with several merchant status providers to determine the most appropriate and cost-effective equipment for your business.

> ## Bright Idea
> Some mailers prefer stamps because they look more personal; others prefer metered mail because it looks more corporate. Make your decision based on your style and the image you want to create for your company.
>
> *Suggestion:* Use metered mail for invoices, statements, and other official business, and use stamps for thank-you notes and similar marketing correspondence that could use a personal touch.

Telecommunications

The ability to communicate quickly with your clients and suppliers is essential to any business. Also, if you have employees who telecommute or if you use home-based

Business Support Service Supply Checklist

You will need to see if you really need all of these items, but our research found that most owners had these tools in their offices:

Items	Price
❑ Broadband internet access	$_____
❑ Business card scanner	$_____
❑ CD ROM	$_____
❑ CD/RW	$_____
❑ Digital camera	$_____
❑ DVD ROM	$_____
❑ Fax machine	$_____
❑ Firewall security	$_____
❑ Flatbed scanner	$_____
❑ Notary stamp (if you are a notary)	$_____
❑ PDA	$_____
❑ Photocopier	$_____
❑ Laserjet printer	$_____
❑ Laserjet color printer	$_____
❑ USB drive	$_____
❑ Webcam	$_____
❑ Zip drive	$_____
❑ Phone system	$_____
❑ Answering machine	$_____
❑ Cross cut shredder	$_____
❑ DAT backup drive	$_____
❑ Transcription equipment (only if you offer these services)	$_____

Don't run out and buy everything on this list, but keep it in your planning folder in case you need to budget for it later.

Office Supplies Checklist

Use this handy list as a shopping guide for equipping your office with supplies (you probably already have some of these). After you've done your shopping, fill in the purchase price next to each item, add up your costs, and you'll have a head start on estimating your start-up costs. Of course, this is not a complete list of supplies that you may need, so tailor it to what you think you will use.

Items	Price
❏ Scratch pads	$_____
❏ Staplers, staples, and staple removers	$_____
❏ Tape and dispensers	$_____
❏ Scissors	$_____
❏ "Sticky" notes in an assortment of sizes	$_____
❏ Paper clips	$_____
❏ Plain paper for your copier and printer	$_____
❏ Paper and other supplies for your fax machine	$_____
❏ Letter openers	$_____
❏ Pens, pencils, and holders	$_____
❏ Correction fluid (to correct typewritten or handwritten documents)	$_____
❏ Trash cans	$_____
❏ Desktop document trays	$_____
❏ Labels	$_____
Total Office Supplies Expenditures:	$_____

independent contractors, being able to reach them quickly is important. Advancing technology gives you a wide range of telecommunications options. Most telephone companies have created departments dedicated to small and homebased businesses; contact your local service provider and ask to speak with someone who can review your needs and help you put together a service and equipment package that will work for you. Specific elements to keep in mind include:

▲

- *Telephone.* Whether you're homebased or in a commercial location, a single voice telephone line should be adequate during the start-up period. As you grow and your call volume increases, you'll add more lines. However, even if you're homebased, you should have a separate line for your business, and you may want to consider another separate line for your fax and data line.

  Your telephone itself can be a tremendous productivity tool, and most of the models on the market today are rich in features that you will find useful. Such features include automatic redial, which redials the last number you called at regular intervals until the call is completed; programmable memory for storing frequently called numbers; and a speakerphone for hands-free use. You may also want call forwarding, which allows you to forward calls to another phone number when you are not at your desk, and call waiting, which signals you that another call is coming in while you are on the phone. These services are typically available through your telephone company for a monthly fee.

  If you're going to be spending a great deal of time on the phone, perhaps doing marketing or handling customer service, consider a headset for comfort and efficiency. A cordless phone lets you move around freely while talking, but these units vary widely in price and quality, so research them thoroughly before making a purchase.

- *Answering machine/voice mail.* Because your business phone should never go unanswered, you need some sort of reliable answering device to take calls when you can't do it yourself. Whether you buy an answering machine (expect to pay $40 to $150 for one that is suitable for a business), or use the voice-mail service provided through your telephone company is a choice you must make depending on your personal preferences, work style, and needs.

- *Cell phone service.* Your cell phone is your lifeline to your business whenever you are away from your desk. You will want to pick a rate plan that supports your call volume and a service provider that has strong cell service in your area. Not much is worse than dropping a call with a client when they thought you were at your office. Some of the top-of-the-line phones now offer online services such as e-mail and internet access. Don't go for a fancy phone if you aren't going to use all of the extra added features.

- *Toll-free number.* Most business support services are local operations, but if you are planning to build a large operation or are in a niche business and targeting a customer base outside your local calling area, consider a toll-free number so clients can reach you without having to make a long-distance call. Most long-distance service providers offer toll-free numbers, and they have a wide range of service and price packages. Shop around to find the best deal.

Reference Materials

Your clients will expect you to know or be able to find the answer to any grammar or formatting question, so a good set of reference materials is essential. You'll need a good dictionary, style guide, and desk reference. (See the Appendix for suggested titles.) You'll also want to own additional reference sources, depending on the special needs of your clients. For example, if you prepare a lot of manuscripts, you'll want a guide for that. If you type research papers or reports, you'll want a good general reference book along with the guidelines of the institution(s) your clients are submitting papers to. If your target market is a particular industry, find a book that lists terminology along with presentation tips that are appropriate.

8

Business
Structure

There's a lot more to starting a business support service than having a computer and being able to type. This chapter will discuss the various issues you need to consider when you're setting up.

Naming Your Company

Your company name can be an important marketing tool. A well-chosen name can work very hard for you; an ineffective name means you have to work much harder at marketing your firm and letting people know what you have to offer. Check out the Business Name Brainstorming Worksheet on page 87 for strategies to help you develop your business name.

Regardless of what type of business you're in, your company name should very clearly identify what you do in a way that will appeal to your target market. It should be short, catchy, and memorable. It should also be easy to pronounce and spell—people who can't say your company name may still use you, but they won't refer you to anyone else.

Many business support service owners simply use their own name and the primary service they provide, such as Voss Transcriptions Inc. A similar approach is to use some sort of regional or other descriptive designation, plus the primary service category offered, as one of the entrepreneurs we interviewed did.

You might want to get clever. Consider WordCare, the name of another entrepreneur's company. The entrepreneur and his wife made a list of words related to the services they wanted to offer (word processing, office support, resumes, desktop publishing) and then began playing with various combinations until the came up with one they liked. "This one just fit, and I like the name," the entrepreneur says. "The only thing I don't like about it is that I'm at the bottom of the list in the Yellow Pages, but we figured it was a good enough name that it was worth it. And we've gotten good feedback on the name."

Check out your competition in the area. What do you like about other names and how can you make your business name stand out? Check out the Appendix for current business support services across the country to get ideas for your business.

You may decide that your business doesn't even need a name. One of the entrepreneurs we spoke with works essentially as an independent contractor under her own name and doesn't use a business name. "It's easier that way," she says.

Take a systematic approach to naming your company. Once you've decided on two or three possibilities, take the following steps.

> ## Bright Idea
>
> When naming your company, consider creating a word that doesn't exist—that's what companies like Exxon and Kodak did. Just be sure the syllables blend to make an ear-appealing sound and that the name is simple enough for people to remember. Also, check to make sure you haven't inadvertently come up with a name that means (or even implies) something negative in another language.

Business Name Brainstorming Worksheet

List three ideas based on the services you plan to provide (e.g. desktop publishing, transcription services, temporary staffing services, etc.):

1. _____

2. _____

3. _____

List three ideas based on your special niche (e.g. transcription services for medical centers, desktop publishing for church newsletters, webpage design for small businesses, etc.):

1. _____

2. _____

3. _____

List three ideas combining a favorite theme with your special niche (Table for Two menu designs, etc.):

1. _____

2. _____

3. _____

After you have decided which name you like best, ask yourself a few important questions:

○ Have you said it aloud to make sure it's easily understood and pronounced?

○ Have you checked to make sure that the name is not already used locally or if a similar name is taken?

○ Have you checked with your local business authority to make sure the name is available?

○ Have you started your trademark search?

- *Check the name for effectiveness and functionality.* Does it quickly and easily convey what you do? Is it easy to say and spell? Is it memorable in a positive way? Ask several of your friends and associates to serve as a focus group to help you evaluate the name's impact.

- *Search for potential conflicts in your local market.* Find out if any other local or regional business serving your market area has a name so similar that yours might confuse the public.

- *Check for legal availability.* Exactly how you do this depends on the legal structure you choose. Typically, sole proprietorships and partnerships operating under a name other than that of the owner(s) are required by the county, city, or state to register their fictitious name. Even if it's not required, it's a good idea, because that means no one else can use that name. Your bank or local newspaper may be able to help you file for a fictitious name. Corporations usually operate under their corporate name. In either case, you need to check with the appropriate regulatory agency to be sure the name you choose is available.

- *Check for use on the internet.* If someone else is already using your name as a domain, consider coming up with something else. Even if you have no intention of developing a web site of your own, the use could be confusing to your customers.

- *Check to see if the name conflicts with any name listed on your state's trademark register.* Your state Department of Commerce can either help you or direct you to the correct agency. You should also check with the trademark register maintained by the U.S. Patent and Trademark Office (PTO).

Once the name you've chosen passes these tests, you need to protect it by registering it with the appropriate state agency; again, your state Department of Commerce can help you. Though most business support services are local operations, if you expect to be doing business on a national level, you should also register the name with the PTO.

Legal Structure

One of the first decisions you'll need to make about your new business is the legal structure of your company. This is an important decision, and it can affect your financial liability, the amount of taxes you pay, the degree of ultimate control you have over the company, as well as your ability to raise money, attract investors, and ultimately sell the business. However, legal structure shouldn't be confused with operating structure. Attorney Robert S. Bernstein, managing partner with Bernstein Bernstein Krawec & Wymard, P.C., explains the difference: "The legal structure is the ownership structure—who actually owns the company. The operating structure defines who makes management decisions and runs the company."

A sole proprietorship is owned by the proprietor; a partnership is owned by the partners; and a corporation is owned by the shareholders. Another business structure is the limited liability company (LLC), which combines the tax advantages of a sole proprietorship with the liability protection of a corporation. The rules on LLCs vary by state; check with your state's Department of Corporations for the latest requirements.

Sole proprietorships and partnerships can be operated however the owners choose. In a corporation, the shareholders typically elect directors, who in turn elect officers, who then employ other people to run and work in the company. But it's entirely possible for a corporation to have only one shareholder and to essentially function as a sole proprietorship. In any case, how you plan to operate the company should not be a major factor in your choice of legal structures.

So what goes into choosing a legal structure? The first point, says Bernstein, is who is actually making the decision on the legal structure. If you're starting the company by yourself, you don't need to take anyone else's preferences into consideration. "But if there are multiple people involved, you need to consider how you're going to relate to each other in the business," he says. "You also need to consider the issue of asset protection and limiting your liability in the event things don't go well."

Something else to think about is your target customers and what their perception will be of your structure. While it's not necessarily true, Bernstein says, "There is a tendency to believe that the legal form of a business has some relationship to the sophistication of the owners, with the sole proprietor as the least sophisticated and the corporation as the most sophisticated." If your target market is going to be other businesses, it might enhance your image if you incorporate. Your image notwithstanding, the biggest advantage of forming a corporation is in the area of asset protection, which, says Bernstein, is the process of making sure that the assets which you don't want to put into the business don't stand liable for the business's

Beware!

Find out what type of licenses and permits are required for your business while you're still in the planning stage. You may find out that you can't legally operate the business you're envisioning, so give yourself time to make adjustments to your strategy before you've spent a lot of time and money trying to move in an impossible direction.

▲

Corporate Checklist

If you are going to incorporate, make sure your corporation stays on the right side of the law and pay attention to these guidelines:

❑ Call the Secretary of State each year to check your corporate status.

❑ Put the annual meetings on tickler cards.

❑ Check all contracts to ensure the proper name is used on each. The signature line should read "John Doe, President, XYZ Corp." never just "John Doe."

❑ Never use your name followed by DBA (doing business as) on a contract. Renegotiate any old ones that do.

❑ Before undertaking any activity out of the normal course of business—like purchasing major assets—write a corporate resolution permitting it. Keep all completed forms in the corporate book.

❑ Never use corporate checks for personal debts and vice versa.

❑ Get professional advice about continued retained earnings not needed for immediate operating expenses.

❑ Know in advance what franchise fees are due (if applicable).

Source: Entrepreneur Magazine's *Start Your Own Business.*

debt. However, to take advantage of the protection a corporation offers, you must respect the corporation's identity. That means maintaining the corporation as a separate entity; keeping your corporate and personal funds separate, even if you are the sole shareholder; and following your state's rules regarding holding annual meetings and other record-keeping requirements.

Is any one of these structures better than another? No. We found business support services operating as sole proprietors, partners, and corporations, and they made their choices based on what was best for their particular situation, which is what you should do. For example, Joann Voss worked for ten years as a sole proprietor, and then, on the advice of her attorney, incorporated in 1994 after winning a large contract.

Do you need an attorney to set up a corporation or a partnership? Again, no. Bernstein says there are plenty of good do-it-yourself books and kits on the market, and most of the state agencies that oversee corporations have guidelines you can use. Even so, it's always a good idea to have a lawyer at least look over your documents before you file them, just to make sure they are complete and will allow you to truly function as you want to.

Finally, remember that your choice of legal structure is not an irrevocable decision, although if you're going to make a switch, it's easier to go from the simpler forms to the more sophisticated ones than the other way around. Bernstein says the typical pattern is to start as a sole proprietor, and then move up to a corporation as the business grows. But if you need the asset protection of a corporation from the beginning, start out that way. Says Bernstein, "If you're going to the trouble to start a business, decide on a structure and put it all together. It's worth the extra effort to make sure it's really going to work."

Licenses and Permits

Most cities and counties require business operators to obtain various licenses and permits to comply with local regulations. While you are still in the planning stages, check with your local planning and zoning department or city/county business license department to find out what licenses and permits you will need and how to obtain them. You may need some or all of the following:

- *Occupational license or permit.* This is typically required by the city (or county if you are not within an incorporated city) for just about every business operating within its jurisdiction. License fees are essentially a tax, and the rates vary widely, based on the location and type of business. As part of the application process, the licensing bureau will check to make sure there are no zoning restrictions prohibiting you from operating.

- *Fire department permit.* If your business is open to the public, you may be required to have a permit from the local fire department.

- *Sign permit.* Many cities and suburbs have sign ordinances that restrict the size, location, and sometimes the lighting and type of sign you can use in front of your business. Landlords may also impose their own restrictions. Most residential areas forbid signs altogether. To avoid costly mistakes, check regulations and secure the written approval of your landlord before you invest in a sign.

- *State licenses.* Many states require persons engaged in certain occupations to hold licenses or occupational permits. Often, these people must pass state examinations before they can conduct business. States commonly require licensing for auto mechanics, plumbers, electricians, building contractors, collection agents, insurance agents, real estate brokers, repossessors, and personal service providers such as doctors, nurses, barbers, cosmetologists, etc. It is unlikely that you'll need a state license to operate your business support service, but it's a good idea to check with your state's occupation licensing entity to be sure.

Just the Tax, Ma'am

Laws regarding the collection and remittance of sales tax vary by state, so you need to check with your state's Department of Revenue to see what you're required to do. Many states treat products and services differently when it comes to sales tax; for example, you may not be required to charge tax on your word-processing fees, but you might have to collect sales tax on labels you print for your customers.

Typically, you'll be required to file your state sales tax return quarterly, but this varies by state and can often be negotiated based on your volume. If you are in a state that does not tax services, and your taxable sales are likely to be limited to a very small amount of office supplies, you may even be allowed to file annually.

Whatever you do, don't be careless about sales tax. Failing to properly collect and remit sales tax is a serious crime with very unpleasant consequences.

Business Insurance

It takes a lot to start a business—even a small one—so protect your investment with adequate insurance. If you are homebased, don't assume your homeowners' or renters' policy covers your business equipment; chances are, it doesn't. If you're located in a commercial facility, be prepared for your landlord to require proof of certain levels of liability insurance when you sign the lease. And in either case, you need coverage for your equipment, supplies, clients' materials, and other valuables.

A smart approach to insurance is to find an agent who works with other professional services businesses. The agent should be willing to help you analyze your needs, evaluate the risks you're willing to accept, and the risks you need to insure against, and work with you to keep your insurance costs down.

Typically, homebased business support services will want to make sure their equipment and supplies are insured against theft and damage by a covered peril, such as fire or flood, and that they have some liability protection if someone (either a customer or an employee) is injured on

> **Tip...**
>
> **Smart Tip**
> When you purchase insurance on your equipment and inventory, ask what documentation the insurance company requires before you have to file a claim. That way, you'll be sure to maintain appropriate records, and the claims process will be easier if it is ever necessary.

their property. In most cases, one of the new insurance products designed for homebased businesses will provide sufficient coverage. Also, if you use your vehicle for business, be sure it is adequately covered.

If you opt for a commercial location, your landlord will probably require certain levels of general liability coverage as part of the terms of your lease. You'll also want to cover your supplies, equipment, and fixtures. Once your business is up and running, consider business interruption insurance to replace lost revenue and cover related costs if you are ever unable to operate due to covered circumstances.

Although it's not extremely common in the business support service industry, you may have clients who want to see a certificate of insurance or who want to be listed as an insured on your liability coverage. Your insurance agent should be able to help you with this paperwork.

The insurance industry is responding to the special needs of small businesses by developing affordable products that provide coverage on equipment, liability, and even loss of income. Bill Pypes says his small-business package gives him the coverage he needs for peace of mind at a nominal fee.

Professional Services

As a business owner, you may be the boss, but you can't be expected to know everything. You'll occasionally need to turn to professionals for information and assistance. It's a good idea to establish a relationship with these professionals before you get into a crisis situation.

To shop for a professional service provider, ask your friends and associates for recommendations. You might also check with your local chamber of commerce or trade association for referrals. Find someone who understands your industry and specific business and appears eager to work with you. Check them out with the Better Business Bureau and the appropriate state licensing agency before committing yourself.

▲

As a business support service owner, the professional service providers you're likely to need include:

- *Attorney.* You need a lawyer who practices in the area of business law, is honest, and appreciates your patronage. In most parts of the United States, there are many lawyers willing to compete fiercely for the privilege of serving you. Interview several and choose one you feel comfortable with. Be sure to clarify the fee schedule ahead of time, and get your agreement in writing. Keep in mind that good commercial lawyers don't come cheap; if you want good advice, you must be willing to pay for it. Your attorney should review all contracts, leases, letters of intent, and other legal documents before you sign them. He or

---

Cover Me

Errors and omissions (E&O) insurance protects you in the event you make a mistake that causes damage to a client. Whether or not you need this particular coverage depends on the type of work you're doing.

For the most part, claims an industry expert, the business support service industry falls under the trade custom of the printing industry (final proofreading is the responsibility of the client, and your liability is limited to providing a corrected draft of the project, and not to any subsequent printing, postage, or loss-of-business aspects of the situation, such as an inaccurate phone number or date). Even so, you should remind your clients of this custom and urge them to proofread the work carefully before using it in any way. It's also a good idea to have clients sign and date their approval of drafts, particularly when the project is critical or a mistake could be costly.

Because of this trade custom, the need for errors and omissions insurance may be considered necessary only for medical transcription and perhaps legal transcription, says the expert. We recommend those two areas because these clients—doctors and attorneys—are the ones most likely to be sued capriciously, and it's hard for the outside service provider to stay out of the litigious loop once it begins. Having E&O insurance may help reduce financial and other inconveniences during litigation.

E&O insurance may also be something to consider if you offer services outside what is considered standard business support services (word processing, desktop publishing, database management, etc.), where your client has the opportunity to check and approve the final product. If you offer any type of consulting, research services, web site design, or other professional service, you may want to protect yourself with E&O coverage.

---

she can also help you with collecting bad debts and establishing personnel policies and procedures. Of course, if you are unsure of the legal ramifications of any situation, call your attorney immediately.

- *Accountant.* Among your outside advisors, your accountant is likely to have the greatest impact on the success or failure of your business. If you are forming a corporation, your accountant should counsel you on tax issues during start-up. On an ongoing basis, your accountant can help you organize the statistical data concerning your business, assist in charting future actions based on past performance, and advise you on your overall financial strategy regarding purchasing, capital investment, and other matters related to your business goals. A good accountant will also serve as a tax advisor, making sure you are in compliance with all applicable regulations and that you don't overpay any taxes.

- *Insurance agent.* A good independent insurance agent can assist with all aspects of your business insurance, from general liability to employee benefits, and probably even handle your personal lines, as well. Look for an agent who works with a wide range of insurers and understands your particular business. This agent should be willing to explain the details of various types of coverage, consult with you to determine the best coverage, help you understand the degree of risk you are taking, work with you in developing risk-reduction programs, and assist in expediting any claims.

- *Banker.* You need a business bank account and a relationship with a banker. Don't just choose the bank you've always done your personal banking with; it may not be the best bank for your business. Interview several bankers before making a decision on where to place your business. Once your account is opened, maintain a relationship with the banker. Periodically sit down and review your accounts and the services you use to make sure you are getting the package most appropriate for your situation. Ask for advice if you have financial questions or problems. When you need a loan or a bank reference to provide to creditors, the relationship you've established will work in your favor.

- *Consultants.* The consulting industry is booming, and for good reason. Consultants can provide valuable, objective input on all aspects of your business. Consider hiring a business consultant to evaluate your business plan or a marketing consultant to assist you in that area. When you are ready to hire employees, a

> **Tip...**
>
> **Smart Tip**
>
> Not all attorneys are created equal, and you may need more than one. For example, the lawyer who can best guide you in contract negotiations may not be the most effective counsel when it comes to employment issues. Ask about areas of expertise and specialization before retaining a lawyer.

human resources consultant may help you avoid some costly mistakes. Consulting fees vary widely, depending on the individual's experience, location, and field of expertise. If you can't afford to hire a consultant, consider contacting the business school at the nearest college or university and hiring an MBA student to help you.

- *Computer expert.* Your computer is your most valuable physical asset, so if you don't know much about computers, find someone to help you select a system and the appropriate software, who will be available to help you maintain, trouble-shoot, and expand your system as you need it.

Most of the business owners we talked with have ongoing relationships with accountants and know of an attorney they can call on if they need one. They also have other advisors. For example, Joann Voss' sister owns an insurance agency, so Joann turns to her for advice on insurance issues and general business management issues.

Creating Your Own Advisory Board

Not even the president of the United States is expected to know everything. That's why he surrounds himself with advisors—experts in particular areas who provide knowledge and information to help him make decisions. Savvy small-business owners use a similar strategy.

You can assemble a team of volunteer advisors to meet with you periodically to offer advice and direction. Because this isn't an official or legal entity, you have a great deal of latitude in how you set it up. Advisory boards can be structured to help with the direct operation of your company and to keep you informed on various business, legal, and financial trends that may affect you. Use these tips to set up your advisory board:

- *Structure a board that meets your needs.* Generally, you'll want a legal advisor, an accountant, a marketing expert, a human resources person, and perhaps a financial advisor. You may also want successful entrepreneurs from other industries who understand the basics of business and will view your operation with a fresh eye.

- *Ask the most successful people you can find, even if you don't know them well.* You'll be surprised at how willing people are to help another business succeed.

- *Be clear about what you are trying to do.* Let your prospective advisors know what your goals are and that you don't expect

> "One of my biggest mistakes was not asking enough questions, not asking for help from organizations like SCORE, and not having a mentor."
>
> —Michelle Ulrich,
> The Virtual Nation

them to take on an active management role or to assume any liability for your company or for the advice they offer.

- *Don't worry about compensation.* Advisory board members are rarely compensated with more than lunch or dinner. Of course, if a member of your board provides a direct service—for example, if an attorney reviews a contract or an accountant prepares a financial statement—then they should be paid at their normal rate. But that's not part of their job as an advisory board member. Keep in mind that, even though you don't write them a check, your advisory board members will likely benefit in a variety of tangible and non-tangible ways. Being on your board will expose them to ideas and perspectives they may not otherwise see and will also expand their own network.

- *Consider the group dynamics when holding meetings.* You may want to meet with all the members together, or in small groups of one or two. It all depends on how they relate to each other and what you need to accomplish.

- *Ask for honesty, and don't be offended when you get it.* Your pride might be hurt when someone points out something you're doing wrong, but the awareness will be beneficial in the long run.

- *Learn from failure as well as success.* Encourage board members to tell you about their mistakes so you can avoid making them.

- *Respect the contribution your board members are making.* Let them know you appreciate how busy they are, and don't abuse or waste their time.

- *Make it fun.* You are, after all, asking these people to donate their time, so create a pleasant atmosphere.

- *Listen to every piece of advice.* Stop talking and listen. You don't have to follow every piece of advice, but you need to hear it.

- *Provide feedback to the board.* Good or bad, let the board know what you did and what the results were.

9

Start-Up
Economics

We've discussed the requirements of setting up a business and now we need to add up the costs. One of the most appealing aspects of the business support service industry is its relatively low start-up costs. If you have a decent credit rating, you can be ready to start serving clients with virtually no cash out of pocket—although you'll certainly be on

▲

firmer ground if you have some start-up capital. But whether all you have is a credit card or you've got a nice fat savings account ready to invest, opening your doors is only part of the financial picture.

Stat Fact
Of our 40 surveyed entrepreneurs, 78 percent started their businesses on less than $2,000 and 90 percent of them started with less than $5,000.

The issue of money has two sides: How much do you need to start and operate, and how much can you expect to take in? Doing this analysis is often extremely difficult for small-business owners who would rather be in the trenches getting the work done than bound to a desk dealing with tiresome numbers, which is why we have provided the Personal Balance Sheet on page 101.

Most of the business support service entrepreneurs we talked with used their own personal savings and equipment they already owned to start their businesses. Because the start-up costs are relatively low, you'll find traditional financing difficult to obtain—banks and other lenders would much rather lend amounts much larger than you'll need and are likely to be able to qualify for.

Many operators start their businesses on the side while working full-time jobs, so their personal living expenses are covered. But if you plan to plunge into your new business full-time from the start, be sure you have enough cash on hand to cover your expenses until the revenue starts coming in. At a minimum, you should have the equivalent of three months' expenses in a savings account to tap if you need it; you'll probably sleep better if you have six to 12 months of expenses socked away.

As you're putting together your financial plan, consider these sources of start-up funds:

- *Your own resources.* Do a thorough inventory of your assets. People generally have more assets than they immediately realize. This could include savings accounts, equity in real estate, retirement accounts, vehicles, recreation equipment, collections, and other investments. You may opt to sell assets for cash or use them as collateral for a loan. Take a look, too, at your personal line of credit; most of the equipment you'll need is available through retail stores that accept credit cards.

- *Friends and family.* The logical next step after gathering your own resources is to approach your friends and relatives who believe in you and want to help you succeed. Be cautious with these arrangements; no matter how close you are, present yourself professionally, put everything in writing, and be sure the individuals you approach can afford to take the risk of investing in your business.

- *Partners.* Though most business support services are owned by just one person, you may want to consider using the "strength in numbers" principle and look around for someone who may want to team up with you in your venture. You may choose someone who has financial resources and wants to

Personal Balance Sheet

By filling out a personal balance sheet, you will be able to determine your net worth. Finding your net worth early on is an important step in becoming a business owner.

Assets	Totals
Cash and checking	
Savings accounts	
Real estate/home	
Automobiles	
Bonds	
Securities	
Insurance cash values	
Other	
Total Assets A	
Liabilities	**Totals**
Current monthly bills	
Credit card/charge account bills	
Mortgage	
Auto loans	
Finance company loans	
Personal debts	
Other	
Total Liabilities B	
Net Worth (A – B = C) C	
Degree of Indebtedness	
Total Liabilities B	
Total Assets A	
Degree of Indebtedness D	

Source: Entrepreneur Magazine's Start Your Own Business

work side-by-side with you in the business. Or you may find someone who has money to invest but no interest in doing the actual work. Be sure to create a written partnership agreement that clearly defines your respective responsibilities and obligations.

- *Government programs.* Take advantage of the abundance of local, state, and federal programs designed to support small businesses. Make your first stop the U.S. Small Business Administration; then investigate various other programs. Women, minorities, and veterans should check out niche financing possibilities designed to help these groups get into business. The business section of your local library is a good place to begin your research.

How Much Do You Need?

So what do you need in the way of cash and available credit to open your doors? Depending on what you already own, the services you want to offer, and whether you'll be homebased or in a commercial location, that number could range from a few hundred to thousands of dollars.

Charlene Davis decided to invest in a new computer and printer and says she spent about $3,500 on equipment and supplies to get started.

Entrepreneur Bill Pypes and his wife used credit to buy the company's first computer and printer and managed to get up and running with a cash outlay of less than $1,000. Because he was a student at the time, he bought and financed his computer at a discount (total cost of about $2,500) through the university; most of the initial cash was spent on marketing.

As you consider your own situation, don't pull a start-up number out of the air; use your business plan to calculate how much you will need to start your ideal operation, and then figure out how much you have. If you have all the cash you need, you are very fortunate. If you don't, you need to start playing with the numbers and start deciding what you can do without.

The Start-Up Budget Guide on page 103 is a sample brainstorming guide. Prices are estimated ranges and will vary depending on features, sources, and whether they are new or used. Ranges beginning with $0 are either optional or items you're likely to already own and therefore don't need to purchase.

 Beware!
Most of the equipment you need can be purchased at a retail store and charged on a credit card—but too much debt can doom your business before it gets off the ground. Only use your credit cards for items that will contribute to revenue generation, and have a repayment plan in place before you buy.

Start-Up Budget Guide

Item	Price Range
Computer system (including printer)	$2,000–4,500
Typewriter	$0–500
Fax machine	$100–600
Accounting/billing software	$75–300
Other software	$0–2,000
Phone system	$0–500
Answering machine	$0–150
Uninterruptible power supply	$90–200
Zip drive	$100–150
Tape transcription machine	$150–300
Surge protector	$30–150
Calculator	$0–100
Copier	$200–500
Desk and chair	$0–1,000
Printer stand	$50–150
File cabinet(s)	$50–500
Bookcase(s)	$30–150
Computer/copier paper	$0–25
Stationery (business cards, letterhead, envelopes)	$75–400
Address stamp	$5–25
Extra printer cartridge	$75–150
Extra fax cartridge	$30–70
Miscellaneous office supplies	$0–200

Pricing Your Services

You have a number of options when it comes to deciding on your approach to pricing. Some operators simply call around, find out what other companies are charging, and set their prices in that range. Others decide what they want to earn and set their prices based on that without regard to how it relates to the competition. Then there's the issue of pricing by the project, the page, or the hour.

One approach is a multifaceted one that considers the skill level of the work, your profit goals, and the market. You need to set up a system that gives you a structure to work within so you can quote consistent, reasonable, and fair rates.

Beware!

If you use subcontractors, be sure the difference between what you pay them and what you're charging your client is great enough so your profit will be worthwhile. When you subcontract to other business support services, you may find them willing to offer a discount—to essentially "wholesale" their services to you, and you "retail" the finished work to the client. In any case, if you can't make a profit, subcontracting is a waste of time.

Multiple Hourly Rates

If you're going to charge by the hour, consider that different rates should apply depending on the complexity of the service and skill level required.

An hourly pricing structure could look something like this:

- *Level 1* (lowest hourly rate). Basic word processing, routine clerical services, simple proofreading
- *Level 2*. Enhanced word processing, copy editing, proofreading, basic spreadsheet design, internet research
- *Level 3*. Desktop publishing, spreadsheet design, simple web page design, simple Web page maintenance
- *Level 4*. Graphic design, writing (academic, business, resume, technical), web page design, web page maintenance
- *Level 5* (highest hourly rate). Consulting, training

Note that the same basic task might fall into more than one pricing level, and you'll need to make a judgment call based on the particular project as to which rate to apply.

Some service owners take on a limited clientele base and charge retainer rates. One well-known successful entrepreneur gave us her rates:

- *Retainer Package A*: 12 hours, $85 an hour with a three-month commitment
- *Retainer Package B*: 20 hours, $75 an hour with a three-month commitment

- *Retainer Package C*: 30 hours, $70 an hour with a three-month commitment

A press release is $250 and includes submission to free online sources.

No additional charge for rush jobs.

We have done some of the "asking around" for you and the business support service owners we talked to said:

- "I have one retainer price and that's $60/hour. I do not do rush jobs."

Beware!

Periodically check on what the competition is charging. How? Call and ask. Most will tell you—and though some won't, you'll still get enough to ensure your fees are competitive, but not significantly over or under where the general market is.

- "I offer three pricing structures: hourly, project, and retainer plans. Rush, weekend, and emergency after-hour services are available but require a 25 percent markup charge."

- "Every client and their needs are unique. I prefer to advise clients of my pricing as they approach me, and I generally charge more for rush jobs."

- "I charge $45–$50/hour and I don't usually do rush jobs."

- "I called around to temp agencies to see what they were charging and then figured out what my services were worth. Rush job charge is $40 an hour."

Can I Quote You?

One of the first questions prospective clients ask will likely deal with fees. Avoid quoting a price too soon. This is a smart strategy for two primary reasons:

1. You really do need to be sure you understand the full scope of the work involved so you can quote an accurate and fair price, as well as be sure it's something you are qualified and willing to do.

2. By talking to the prospect about the work, you'll have the opportunity to impress them with your knowledge and professionalism—as well as get to know them so you can decide if they're someone you want to work with.

So when someone asks about price, simply say something like "I want to be sure the estimate I give you is accurate and complete, so before I calculate a fee, may I ask you some questions about the work?" If the client doesn't want to answer your questions, that's a red flag that this is someone who either isn't a serious prospect or will be difficult to work with.

- "My flat rate is $35/hour, but I offer a retainer rate of $33/hour. Since I work on retainer for many, there aren't many rush jobs so I don't have an additional rate."
- "I offer retainer arrangements for clients of 10, 20, or 30 hours per month for a discounted fee, otherwise I offer an hourly fee. A rush job required within 24 hours is charged 1.5 times the hourly rate."
- "I charge an hourly rate for most work and the time is tracked for each client. The minimum charge is 15 minutes. Rush work is charged double the hourly rate."

Remember, each business support service owner offered vastly different skills and services, so use this information to give you an idea of what is being charged in the marketplace. Once you have specified which services you will offer, you will need to tailor your prices to your expertise and deliverable product.

Estimating the Job

Many new business owners find estimating one of the most challenging things they do, but if you approach the process systematically, it's simple. You just need to determine an appropriate hourly rate, calculate the length of time the project should take, and do the math.

Regardless of the format you use to provide the quote (written or verbal), it's a good idea to make notes for yourself so you know what you quoted and how you arrived at that figure. This will be necessary if the actual project turns out to be different from what the client described, or if the client questions the invoice later, even though they agreed to the quote. You may even want to create an estimate form that you can provide to the client and keep a copy in your own files.

Bottom Dollar

You may want to consider setting a minimum—either a dollar amount or an hourly figure—that you bill clients with very small jobs. This takes into consideration the reality that every job requires a certain amount of administrative time (setting up the project, billing, receiving, and processing the payment, etc.), regardless of how small or large the actual project is. So if you bill by the hour, for example, you might have a minimum charge of one hour, regardless of whether the work took you the full hour or just a few minutes. You can, of course, waive the minimum charge for regular clients who give you a substantial amount of work.

Charlene Davis bills by the hour, but she always gives her clients a high-end cap on the project. "I tell them what the hourly rate is, and also how much time I think the project will take," she says. "I want them to have a fair assessment of what it's going to cost them. You can't say 'It's so much an hour, but I don't know how many hours it will take.' If I overestimate the time, then they're happy because they get a bill that's smaller than they anticipated. If I underestimate, I call them as soon as I realize it and we talk about it and work something out." And that last issue brings up another important point about pricing: You need a clear picture of the entire project, and your price quote should include a description of what you understand the project to be in case there's a discrepancy later. "It's beneficial to everyone if the client is honest about the scope of the project from the very beginning," Charlene says.

Joann says many of her clients prefer a page rate, so she has rates for single-spaced and double-spaced pages. She also has an hourly rate. Another business support entrepreneur charges by the page for college papers and resumes, by the hour for businesses, and has a discounted rate for nonprofit organizations.

The Danger of Pricing Too Low

If the client says your quote is too high, consider taking away services to bring the price down—don't just lower the fee. Reducing your rates without any concession from the client says you didn't feel you were worth what you wanted to charge in the first place. Be sure to put the terms in writing so the client doesn't complain later. We have provided an Estimate Form on page 108.

Many new operators take the approach of undercutting existing services as a way to break into the market, but this strategy can backfire.

Industry Production Standards

There is a move in the industry to set prices according to accepted standards rather than based on the actual time it takes someone to do a particular project. The concept makes sense for both the service provider and the client.

Consider this scenario: A client has 90 minutes of audiotape that needs to be transcribed and calls three different services for a quote. The first operator's keyboarding speed is relatively slow, and she is unfamiliar with the client's industry and terminology, so she esti-

> ### Tip...
> **Smart Tip**
> Using production standards to set prices speeds up your estimating process, makes your quotes consistent, and provides you with a tool to measure productivity and profitability.

Estimate Form

Client name: _____

Contact: _____

Address (optional): _____

_____

_____

Phone: _____

Fax: _____

Project description: _____

_____

_____

_____

_____

Fee: $ _____ per hour (or) Total: $ _____

Possible additional services: _____

_____

_____

_____

_____

Fee for additional services: $ _____ per hour (or) Total: $ _____

Estimate provided to client on (date): _____

Price valid until (date): _____

mates that it will take her 7.5 hours to complete the work. The second operator's keyboarding speed is faster, but she is also unfamiliar with the industry and expects to be slowed by terms she hasn't heard before, so she estimates 6.5 hours to complete the work. The third operator types even faster than the second and knows the industry and its jargon well, so she estimates 4.5 hours to transcribe the tape.

If all of these operators are charging at the same hourly rate, the first service would actually make substantially more money even though it doesn't have the skill level or experience as the other two. The third service would actually be penalized for being skilled and knowledgeable.

Using an industry standard to determine the project length and classify its complexity protects clients from excessive time billing by slower service providers and rewards faster service providers for their efficiency—and all the while protects the client by assuring fair pricing.

Bright Idea

Do an annual rate review. Once a year, look at all the fees you charge, and check to make sure the rate is profitable, in line with the market, and fair and reasonable for the service provided. If necessary, make adjustments to your rate.

Marketing Your
Business

Now that you've set up your business, you will need to market it, and this is an area where your creative side can shine. It is something many people don't like to do, but it's essential if you're going to build a successful, profitable business.

Don't be discouraged if your marketing efforts don't produce an immediate response. It's rare that someone will have a need for your services at precisely the moment you contact them, but if you put together a professional, attractive information package, they'll keep the information on file and call you when they need you—or they'll refer you to a colleague who may have the need. It's not unusual for a sales contact not to generate a response for months—or even a year.

> **Stat Fact**
> Of 40 entrepreneurs, 63 percent spend less than $500 a year in marketing, saying that word-of-mouth and networking get them the most business.

There are issues and ideas specific to business support services that you need to know as you develop your marketing plan. For example, check with your local phone company to find out its advertising deadline and directory distribution date and, if possible, plan to launch your business in time to be included. Your Yellow Pages listing will be an important source of new business, especially in the early days, so don't get so distracted by other start-up tasks that you miss this opportunity.

Another important point is to be sure all your marketing materials are professional and letter-perfect. Many business support services that do a great job in this area for their clients often forget to do the same for themselves. Consider hiring a graphic designer and/or professional writer to help you with your marketing package; you may be able to negotiate a trade-out that will benefit you both.

Sharon Williams tells us some successful forms of low-cost marketing for service businesses:

- On and offline networking—network, network, network!
- Emphasize on earning word-of-mouth referrals.
- Join associated business and hobbyist organizations.
- Focus on article marketing by writing free articles to feature your expertise.
- Have a well-structured and informative web site that speaks to your ideal client and identifies the benefits of working with you.
- Create an e-zine or blog and update it frequently with informative and relevant posts.
- Develop a mechanism to capture web site visitor e-mail addresses, so you may pull them into your marketing funnel.

Branding Your Service

Sharon Williams, Chairperson for Alliance for Virtual Businesses also runs her own business support service company, The 24 Hour Secretary. She regularly writes articles for other business support services and entrepreneurs to help them grow their own businesses and she's written this article about the importance of branding your service.

"Branding is often defined as your logo, slogan, tag line, niche, or the one thing that makes your company stand out. Seldom is it described as the 'total package' and how every facet of your company is perceived. But, that's exactly what branding is. Instead of segmenting each component, review your company, beginning with evaluating how you value it and then how you want your customers to perceive it.

What is branding? Branding is the sum of all the images that people have in their heads about a particular company. Using a formula, it is:

Your personal values + the customer's perception about your company
= the lasting memory about your business.

I liken this memory to your making a promise—a promise that isn't easily forgotten because you want your target audience and customers to access this memory whenever they need services.

Promises used to build your brand should include the following:

- The promise of performance
- The promise of benefits
- The promise of personality
- The promise of valued difference
- The promise of a relationship

The purpose of these promises is to convey the benefits of your brand (why a customer should hire you) instead of your competitors.

Is your brand perceived to be unique? To create a substantial advantage in your brand, you must first create uniqueness in the minds of your customers that no other brand can substitute.

Is it important to your core customers? Many business owners believe price is the most important factor in purchases. Studies have shown, however, that it is only one important factor. To win and retain clients you need more, e.g., product mix, service, look, and marketing.

Is your brand sustained with style and substance? Initially, getting clients may be easy, but to retain them entrepreneurs must continuously deliver a superior, recognizable customer benefit.

Creating a memory. Creating a memorable brand is a long-term process predicated on building relationships based on trust, respect, and consistency. It takes time, patience, dedication, and someone who is willing to always fulfill the Brand Promise.

By understanding the fundamentals of constructing a winning brand, developing your 'Promise,' and understanding how it is perceived by your target audience, you can create a lasting memory, increase business and make it very difficult for competitors to compete."

Make Yourself an Expert

Not only do you need to brand your business, but you also need to brand yourself as an expert. One way of doing that is through e-publishing. Below is an article written by Sharon Williams and available on her web site at The24HourSecretary.com:

"E-publishing is fast becoming the preferred method for sharing information by many people around the world. E-books and e-booklets are now given away promotionally or are part of a product line, resulting in increased exposure, profits, and recognition. E-publishing can create leads for new sales, serve informative purposes, be used as a reward for signing up for your service, e-zine, newsletter, or survey. They can be used to solidify you as being an expert in your field. Here are some quick tips to help you win clients using your e-publications.

- *Write what you know.* Choose a topic about which you already have knowledge. This is likely to prompt readers to want more of what you've got.

- *Listen to your e-zine subscribers and customers.* Write about what they want to read. Read their comments and answer their emails personally, professionally, and as soon as possible. If your e-zine reader makes a suggestion you want to use, let them know. Give credit where credit is due.

- *Spelling and grammar.* Use a spell and grammar checker on all e-publications you write, and then read what you wrote again. Ask an associate to review your material. Two sets of eyes are better than one. Your readers may not complain to you, but they will note obvious mistakes, and your credibility may be negatively impacted.

- *Word-of-mouth promotion.* Ask your readers to recommend your e-publications to their friends, family, co-workers, acquaintances, and as many others as possible. Tell them how they will benefit from reading your material. Submit your publication to various e-lists and e-publishing sites. Promote your e-publications online and offline.

- *Try something new.* Find original ideas or subjects. Write about the issues that will keep your customers informed. Your purpose is to find and keep happy customers. Make your publications memorable and a "must read".

- *Be dedicated.* Plan to invest a reasonable amount of time in creating, publishing, and supporting your e-publications. Access your email on a regular basis to respond to inquiries, requests for information, and general customer service.

- *Be consistent*. Give your e-publications format and style an opportunity to work. Too many changes will confuse and frustrate your customers. Test by adding a new section or showcasing a new idea without doing anything drastic.

Have fun: Enjoy creating your e-publications and their content. When it is fun for you, it is usually both fun and more beneficial for your customers."

Referrals Are Essential

Referrals will likely be a primary way you get new clients, so it's a good idea to have a systematic approach to the process. You should be able to identify who is making referrals that ultimately turn into business so you can cultivate and reward those referral sources.

Complementary businesses are great sources of referrals. For example, print and copy shops often have customers who need word processing or desktop publishing but don't have the equipment, skills, or staff to handle these services. By doing the work well, you help them keep a client and make them look good in the process because they were smart enough to know about you.

Your referral arrangements can be set up to provide cash compensation for new business, or you may simply have an agreement where you and other cooperating businesses refer clients to each other as the need arises.

Of course, many referrals involve no compensation at all—satisfied clients will be happy to refer others to you simply because you do a good job. And you'll probably also get referrals from friends and associates. Charlene Davis says a major portion of her company's business came through referrals from people at her church. "Most of my clients over the years have been either church members or people who heard about me from church members or through the church office," she says. "I did some advertising, but I didn't get any results from that. It's all been referrals, most of them directly or indirectly through the church."

You should also build a solid network of referral sources so that when your clients need something you don't do, you have someone you can refer them to. This makes life easier for your clients, who will appreciate you more for it. It also builds a relationship with your referral sources, who will likely return the favor when they can—and may even pay you a referral fee.

Charlene keeps a list of people who provide various business support services so she can give referrals if someone calls with a project she can't handle herself. "I don't expect any sort of referral fee—I'm more concerned with trying to make sure people get their work done," she says.

Beware!

Not every "Yellow Pages" is a local telephone directory your prospective customers use. Industry-specific or geographic directories produced by independent publishers are rarely worth the cost of the ad. Think about where you look when you need something. Better yet, do a survey of your business associates and prospective clients asking them which telephone directory they would use when looking for a service such as the one you provide.

Advertising

Advertising is a great way to bring in new business, but choosing effective media may take some experimentation. Probably the single best place to advertise is in your local Yellow Pages, because that's where people look when they need a service and don't know who to call.

Many communities have more than one telephone directory publisher, so you may need to do some research to determine which directory (or directories) should carry your listing and ad. Bill Pypes says his community has two telephone directories, and he advertises in both.

Don't limit yourself to the telephone directory. Bill does some radio ads on a local news and talk station, and although he can't credit much specific new business to them, he says his current customers do hear and mention the spots. "It's only $100 to $150 per month, and I figure it's worth it to keep my name alive with current customers," he says. He also places ads in the university newspaper classified section and gets a good response from that.

Joann limits her advertising to the Yellow Pages, one trade journal, and a semiannual direct-mail campaign. She used to buy a mailing list for her direct-mail efforts, but she has found it more effective to build her own list using the telephone directory (using the listing categories of her target market) and trade journals (pulling prospects from ads and editorial mentions) as a resource. "We send a brochure and a Rolodex card, with an introduction, prices, and a toll-free number," she says. "The Rolodex card is really useful, because if they don't use it right away, they generally hang onto it. I've gotten calls years later." See the sample direct-mail letter on page 117.

Knocking on Doors

One of the simplest ways to build business and set yourself apart from the competition is to just get out there and be visible. Knock on doors, hand out brochures, go to networking

Bright Idea

Want to try advertising but don't want to spend the money? Ask the print publication or radio station if you can negotiate a trade-out, where you provide services they need (such as word processing or typesetting) in return for ad space.

Direct-Mail Letter

March 18, 200x

Mr. John Doe
Fawnskin Insurance Co.
123 Deer Lane, Suite A
Bucktown, WA 45678

Dear Mr. Doe,

Do you need administrative assistance but don't have enough volume to justify a full-time employee? Do you occasionally have special projects your staffers don't have time to handle? Or do you periodically need a level of software or internet expertise that you don't have in-house?

ABC Secretarial is the answer. We'll take the overload and special projects off your shoulders so you can concentrate on running and growing your business. Our full line of services includes:

- word processing
- spreadsheets
- mailing list management
- desktop publishing
- internet services

Put us on your team, and together we'll both win. The enclosed brochure tells you more about the specific services we provide. I'll be delighted to meet with you at your convenience to discuss how we can help you.

Cordially,

Jane Smith

Jane Smith
President

P.S. Can't think of a need right now? Put the enclosed Rolodex card in your files and keep us in mind should something come up in the future.

Bright Idea

Give your business card to everyone! In fact, give them two—one to keep, and one to share. It's much easier for someone to make a referral if they can just pass your card along. Wherever you are, whether it's a business or social situation, offer your card when you are introduced. This ensures people know your name, what you do, how to reach you—and they will remember it!

events—do whatever it takes to make sure people know about your company and understand what you do.

You can make your calls on the telephone or in person. If you're targeting a small business, ask to speak to the owner. In a larger operation, the human resources manager may be a good place to start. Depending on your own target market, you could ask to speak to the sales manager with the goal of providing administrative support services to the sales staff.

Present your services concisely from the perspective of what they can do for the client. Hand them a brochure and business card (or mail these if you've called on the phone), and ask if you can help them in any way.

You must also stay visible with your existing clientele. You need to keep reminding them that you are the best game in town, so remember to thank them for their business and make sure you're doing everything they want and need.

Trade Shows and Seminars

If you're marketing to other businesses, it will be worth your while to attend trade shows. There are two types of shows—consumer (which focus on home, garden, and other consumer themes) and business-to-business (where exhibitors market their products and services to other companies). Focus on the business-to-business shows.

You don't need to exhibit; in fact, putting together a strong trade show exhibit is probably beyond the budget of most small business support services. But use the shows as a networking opportunity. Stop at each booth with the idea that the exhibitor is a prospective client; if the product is not something you'd ever buy, pick up the salesperson's business card and move on. Remember that exhibitors pay a substantial amount of money to set up at a show, and they're there to get business, not to buy services. Don't waste their time on the exhibit floor if you're not a prospect for them; make your own sales contact later.

Many shows have refreshment areas and scheduled networking events where you can mix and mingle with exhibitors and other attendees. This is a good opportunity to acquire business cards of potential clients.

Don't just stuff the cards into your pocket; when you can, make a few notes on the card to remind yourself of who the person was and whether or not they indicated any need for your services.

After the show, use the cards you collected as sales leads. Send out a letter and/or a brochure (don't bother to take brochures to the show), and then follow up with a telephone call.

Be sure to take plenty of your own business cards. It's a good idea to wear a dress or suit with pockets, put your own business cards in your left pocket, and reserve your right pocket for the cards you collect. That way, you won't risk accidentally giving away someone else's card. And speaking of dress, wear business clothes—just because the show is held at a resort doesn't mean you should dress like you're on vacation. But remember that you'll likely be on your feet all day, so wear comfortable shoes. Don't chew gum or smoke, and avoid alcohol even at cocktail parties—you're there to make a good impression and get new business, not to play.

> **Tip...**
>
> **Smart Tip**
>
> Ask every new client how they found out about you. Make a note of where they heard about you and what kind of business they represent. This will let you know how well your various marketing efforts are working. You can then decide to increase certain programs and eliminate those that either aren't working or are attracting a type of business you don't want.

To find out about shows in your area, call your local chamber of commerce or convention center and ask for a calendar.

Another very effective marketing technique which can be used in conjunction with trade shows or as a separate effort is to offer free seminars and workshops to your prospective clients. Focus, of course, on some of the services you provide, such as writing a resume, putting together a newsletter, or doing effective direct-mail marketing. You can present your information through local business and civic organizations, churches or schools (adult vocational centers, community colleges, and even private institutions) at virtually no cost, and the host group handles the publicity and promotion.

Though it may sound self-defeating to teach people how to do for themselves what you'd really like to do for them for a fee, it isn't. Many people will listen to your advice, realize the work is too challenging for them, call you to do it for them, and happily pay you. Or they may refer someone else to you.

Reading the Classifieds

One of the best ways to start finding clients is to check out "help wanted" ads in various classifieds, online and in local newspapers. If the employer is looking for secretarial, administrative, or support positions, contact them and offer them your services instead of hiring a full-time employee. If they need someone to answer phones or do receptionist work and you run a staffing business support service, then this marketing idea works for you too. A lot of these ads need someone to work on a computer and do various tasks that can be outsourced to a business support service and is your opportunity to show your business's value. Granted, the company posting the ad may not be aware of the benefits of outsourcing, because it may take some time to show the benefits, so send a cover letter with your marketing materials and follow up to see if they have any questions.

You already know that they need help in the areas of service that you provide and most have probably never thought of outsourcing, or aren't quite clear how it would work. Another option is to contact job postings looking for a full-time employee and offer to assist them with the workload until they hire and train someone for the position. Point out the advantages to working with you—experience, skill, reliability, affordability (after all, they only pay you for what you do—not a salary that continues whether you're working or not)—and ask if they have a small project you could handle (paid, of course) as a demonstration of your service.

Extra Marketing Tips

Posting Fliers at Local Colleges

If part of your business support service offering consists of resume writing, word processing, proofreading, or presentation prepping, then an inexpensive marketing idea is to post fliers on the bulletin boards at your local college or university. Make sure it's easy to read and stands out against everything else on the bulletin board (they can get crowded!)—we recommend brightly-colored paper. Design the flier to have all of your information and services on the main part of the flier and put your contact information on the pull-away tabs so that anyone interested can take it with them. Make sure you get permission from the school to post them since some have strict rules. You will need to replace them often since those tabs tend to disappear quickly.

Post an Ad in the College Newspaper

Similar to the idea above, you could also post an ad in the college's newspaper since they are usually pretty inexpensive and will be direct marketing to your target market. Depending on how the paper is run, you may be able to get discount pricing if you want to run the ad continuously.

Trade Services for Ad Space

If you provide desktop publishing services and develop newsletters for associations or organizations, you may be able to offer to trade some of your services for ad space in their newsletter. You will need to work out the details to make sure it's an even exchange, but if their newsletter targets your market, this could be a good regular arrangement.

Create Bookmarks for Your Local Library

If your services are creative and involve design, contact your local library and offer to design bookmarks. Create a couple of different designs, such as one for children's books and another for mystery books, and offer it to the library for free if you could print your contact information on the back. This may be another opportunity to trade services for advertising space such as designing their book club flyers.

Teach Free Workshops and Seminars

If you are offering resume preparation services or creative writing services, you could offer to teach a workshop through local adult community colleges, churches, or non-profits. Oftentimes the attendees will leave the workshop asking for more help or for you to help them with their resume or refer you to a friend who didn't attend. Again, never miss an opportunity to network!

11

Day-to-Day
Operations

So you've set up your office, you've started doing your marketing, and the business is rolling in. Now you need to run your business. Most people start a particular type of business because they enjoy doing that kind of work, and the typical business support service owner is no different.

So you may find it frustrating that a major portion of your time will be spent on tasks other than doing projects for your clients.

In fact, it will be common for you to have days that are extremely busy and you work very hard, but you don't do anything that can be billed to a client.

As a solo operator, expect to spend at least one-fourth of your time on general business management and administration, marketing, purchasing, and billing. The bigger your business, and the more workers you have, the more time you'll spend managing them rather than actually doing the work yourself. Joann Voss hasn't actually transcribed anything herself in years—she has a team of five full-time employees in the office and nearly 50 part-time transcribers who work from their homes.

No matter how small or large your company is, it's critical that you not neglect the administrative side. It won't do you much good if you do the work but never get around to sending out the invoices so you can get paid. Poorly maintained records can get you into trouble with the IRS and other government agencies. And if you aren't marketing on a regular basis, your business will eventually dry up.

Running a business support service takes a lot of energy. It helps if you enjoy people but are also able to work alone or in small groups. You'll need to be able to juggle several projects at the same time, and always make each client feel as though he or she is the most important person to you.

Dollar Stretcher

Form a purchasing group with other business support services to buy large quantities of supplies so you can take advantage of bulk pricing.

---

18 Ways to Reduce Handling Paperwork

Sharon Williams of the Alliance for Virtual Businesses often writes helpful articles for business support services to streamline their businesses. It's easy when you are handling a client's inbox for yours to get piled high, so here are her 18 ways to reduce handling paperwork.

1. Create a block of time during non-prime hours to handle paperwork. Schedule this in your planner and stick to it.

2. Sort through and handle the papers in your in-basket no more than twice a day.

3. Never handle a piece of paper more than once. Avoid the "I'll just put this here for now" habit.

18 Ways to Reduce Handling Paperwork, cont.

4. Throw away previous drafts. They serve no purpose.

5. Limit the length of letters, recommendations, responses, meeting requests, and other correspondence to one page.

6. Ask people if reports they prepare (or you prepare) are really necessary. Prepare them only when needed, not as a regular routine.

7. Do something with every piece of paper that reaches you and put it in its proper place—not just back on the pile.

8. Reduce the number of memos you keep. After all, memos are primarily for short-term information. Record the information you need and toss the memo.

9. Create different file folders:
   - Training file for useful items on personal or professional development
   - Supplier file for information on products and services
   - Invoices to pay
   - Upcoming events to attend

10. Throw out last month's copy of a magazine when this month's copy arrives. If you must save them, only keep a year's worth. Stop subscriptions to magazines and newspapers you don't read anymore. This saves you money as well as time and guilt.

11. When you find items you keep putting off reading, ask, "How likely am I to read this and how valuable is this information?" Throw it out.

12. Extra storage space ends up getting filled up quickly. Try reducing or throwing out extra paperwork collectors. Limit your stacking trays to two: one for incoming papers and the other for outgoing papers.

13. Reduce your credit cards to one per adult, two if you use one for home and one for work. This reduces statements and bill-paying time.

14. Reduce your bank accounts, if you have several. If you find yourself dealing with multiple bank statements every month, this is a good place to start.

15. Pay bills by automatic deduction. Most utility bills can be handled this way.

16. Put all your receipts in a small envelope. Sort through them every month or every quarter.

17. Handle routine requests or tasks immediately whenever you can.

18. Cut back on sending memos. Use a phone call or e-mail instead.

Tracking Inventory

Your inventory will most likely be limited to the supplies you consume and provide to your clients, so inventory management will not be the same challenge it is for a retailer or a manufacturer. Even so, you need to keep track of what you buy and use, and what you have on hand.

Store supplies in a central location that is cool, dry, and away from strong, direct sunlight. Be sure to rotate your stock, using supplies in a first-in, first-out order.

Smart Tip

Tip...

If you realize you've underestimated your workload and you're likely going to miss a deadline, call the client as soon as possible, apologize, and give them a realistic estimate of when the work is going to be done. Don't let them show up at your office to pick up a job that isn't finished.

Decide what inventory items will be billed back to your customers and what items you consider part of your cost of production. For example, you wouldn't likely bill back the cost of regular paper, but if you supply special stationery, envelopes, or labels, it's reasonable to charge your clients for those items. Make notes on the work order of what you use so you don't forget.

Shipping and Receiving

Unless you're going to offer shipping and receiving as a service to your clients, you aren't likely to have to deal with this aspect of business much. However, most business support services offer pickup and delivery. If you're a solo operator, you'll probably just use your personal car to handle this chore. Or you may use a courier service. Should you charge for pickup and delivery? That's a judgment call you'll have to make; some operators do, and some don't. Charlene Davis, for example, doesn't charge for pickup and delivery because her clients are within a few miles' radius of her house, and she combines this task with other errands so she doesn't feel that it's taking a significant amount of time.

Beware!

Never just sign a delivery receipt for packages. Even though you'll get to know your regular driver, always count the packages and do a quick visual inspection for external signs of damage.

Some business support service entrepreneurs make the decision on a per-client basis. But if you're going to charge, be sure you charge enough. For example, if you had one client who agreed to pay your travel time, but you underestimated how long it actually took

Dollar Stretcher

When it comes to freight services, don't pay for more than you need. Most overnight companies offer two or three levels of next-day service— early morning, before noon, and afternoon. The earlier the guaranteed delivery, the higher the cost. If the next afternoon will meet your customer's needs, don't pay for morning delivery. And if the carrier misses its delivery commitment, insist that it honor its guarantee by refunding the charges.

to make the drive, that mistake would reduce your profitability.

Also, as part of your overall service package, you may want to maintain an inventory of basic office supplies and perhaps even specialty papers that you can either use in the process of doing your clients' work or that you may sell outright to them. You can purchase these products in bulk from wholesalers to allow room for a reasonable markup when you sell individual items.

Certainly you won't have the volume to compete with your local office supply house, but you may still want to sell products such as pens, markers, labels, computer disks, paper, and envelopes. You may also want to keep a stock or a catalog of specialty papers for small runs of brochures or special mailings as a cost-effective alternative to four-color, large-quantity printing. Your clients may also appreciate being able to purchase postage stamps from you, rather than having to make a trip to the post office.

If you decide to offer shipping and receiving, chances are most of your shipments will be small enough to be handled by UPS (United Parcel Service), Federal Express, DHL, the United States Postal Service (USPS), and similar companies. Contact the customer service departments of the package and courier companies serving your area to set up an account so they will bill you, and to arrange for regular pickups if you need them. If your clients are shipping large volumes of material, it's likely they'll have their own staff and facilities to handle it.

Your clients may select the carrier they want you to use, or they may leave the choice up to you. If you have chosen the carrier, make sure the freight company has insurance to cover accidents or losses, because if the carrier makes a mistake, is late with a delivery, or loses or damages a package, it could have a negative impact on your relationship with your customers. Choose your freight companies carefully and demand that they perform up to your high standards.

Bright Idea

Set up a system that helps keep the work flowing and the deadlines met. Some operators create a computerized spreadsheet; others simply mark their work on a project board or calendar. The key is to come up with a system that works for you so you can be sure not to over commit yourself.

Smart Tip

Tip...

Whatever services you offer, be sure you do top-quality work. Pay attention to details, meet your deadlines, and be sure the final product is error-free.

Keeping Time Records

Create a work order and file for each project as soon as it comes in the door. Make notes of the dates, the type of work that was done, who did the work, how long it took, and the billing rate that applies. You can use the form on page 131 or create your own. You can use the work order to create your invoice, or attach a copy of it to your invoice.

A work order can be especially useful when you are doing a variety of smaller projects for a client, and the person who actually pays the bills is not the person who requested the work. For example, you might have typed a few letters for the marketing department, but the bookkeeper may need to know more than that to process the invoice. Remember, they can't actually see you do the work, so they want detailed information about what you did.

Making the Rules

In any relationship, it's a good idea to set boundaries so everyone knows what to expect before any problems develop. In business, those boundaries are usually couched in the form of policies. How formal you want to be will depend on your own personal preferences, the size of your business, and your clientele. A sample Policy Statement is provided on page 129. Charlene Davis takes a casual approach to polices, simply giving new clients a verbal explanation of how she operates. Her relationship with her clients is very personal, and while she always does her best to meet their needs, it isn't always possible. "I'm a one-person company, and I don't pretend to be anything else," she says. "When I get a project, I find out when the deadline is, and if I can't meet it, I say so. It may be because I've got other work to do, or I may have personal obligations—whatever. I just say, 'I'm sorry, but I'm not going to be able to turn that around for you in that time frame.' Then we decide if they can live with what I can do, or if they need to take the job somewhere else."

Policies also give your clients some guidelines so that they can make reasonable requests. Many clients seem excessively demanding because they just don't think about what's involved in getting the work done; setting policies that give them choices in pricing and service levels will make your relationship smoother and stronger.

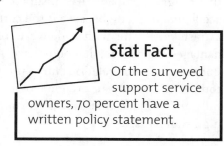

Stat Fact

Of the surveyed support service owners, 70 percent have a written policy statement.

Policy Statement

ABC Business Support Service

1. Standard turnaround time is 24 to 48 hours. (Some projects may require additional time, which will be decided and agreed upon at the time of project drop-off.)

2. Rush rates are available. Any project required in less than 24 hours will be billed at a 50 percent increase.

3. A minimum charge of .5 hours (1/2 hour) will always apply.

4. Time spent with client discussing or reviewing the project will be applicable to ABC Secretarial Service's hourly rate.

5. Payment for all projects is required at time of pickup. If monthly billing is requested, a credit form is available. Monthly billing will not be available until credit references are verified and credit is approved.

6. We will make every effort to locate and correct all errors prior to your review; however, **CLIENT** is responsible for final proof. Our responsibility is limited to providing you with original page(s) only and does not extend to duplicating charges. Therefore, proofread your project carefully **PRIOR** to duplication. Errors or omissions found thereafter are **CLIENT'S** responsibility.

7. Should an electronic copy of your project be required, a five-dollar ($5) fee per document, plus a "disk" charge, will be applied. (Disk charges vary depending on the type of disk required.)

8. ABC's files will be purged one year after completion of project. Should you require longer storage, arrangements must be made in advance and a storage fee will be applied. Should a client return after a project has been purged and storage arrangements have not been made, client shall then be responsible for charges incurred to rekey the entire document.

9. Prices are subject to change without prior notice.

10. All typeset and print work must be signed off by client. Should an error in typesetting be found after print is run, **CLIENT** will be responsible for reprint charges.

If you have any questions regarding the above policies,
please do not hesitate to contact us.
Thank you for choosing ABC Secretarial Service.

▲

"I Do" or "I Don't"?

You don't have to accept every project a client brings you. Here are some questions to ask to help you decide when to say yes—and when to say no.

○ Will you enjoy the work? If you're a solo operator and will be doing the work yourself, is it something you'll enjoy, or will you be miserable?

○ Do you have time to do the job right? Consider this from two angles: Do you want to spend the time, and can you meet the deadline?

○ Will accepting this particular job (or taking on this client) affect your relationship with existing clients?

○ Is there anything questionable about the work in terms of honesty, integrity, or legality?

Firing Clients

Sometimes you'll lose clients because they decide to use another service or do the work themselves, but sometimes you need to take the initiative to "lose" the client yourself—that is, you need to terminate your relationship for whatever reason.

> "My biggest mistake was trying to be all things to all people. I wanted to get that first client and was willing to do anything to get them."
>
> —Lyn Prowse-Bishop, MVA, ASO, Executive Stress Office Support

It may be that the client is simply too demanding—everything is always a rush, they don't care that they are routinely asking you to stay up until all hours to get the work done, or they refuse to consider that you may have other clients who also need service. It may be that they don't pay on time, quibble over fees, or are just unpleasant to deal with for a variety of other reasons.

Beware!

When clients are in a hurry for a project, they may try to pressure you into committing to an unrealistic deadline. Don't give in and promise something that isn't possible—you'll just have a problem later when you are unable to deliver.

Whenever possible, you'll want to salvage the relationship, and you may be able to do that by communicating with the client about the issues that are creating problems. But when all else fails, and a client is causing you more

Work Order

ABC Business Support Service

Name: _____

Company: _____

Street address: _____

City: _____ State: _____ Zip: _____

Phone number: _____ Fax number: _____

Driver's license number: _____

Referred by (previous customer, Yellow Pages, etc.): _____

Estimate: _____

Date/time project dropped off: _____

Date/time project due: _____

Description of project: _____

_____

_____

_____

_____

Additional instructions: _____

_____

_____

We will make every effort to locate and correct all errors prior to your review; however, **CLIENT** *is responsible for final proof. Our responsibility is limited to providing you with original page(s) only and does not extend to duplicating charges. Therefore, proofread your project carefully* **PRIOR** *to duplication. Errors or omissions found thereafter are* **CLIENT'S** *responsibility.*

▲

trouble and misery than the money they're paying you is worth, you should politely but firmly tell them you can't work for them anymore. If you feel comfortable referring them to another service, then by all means do so. But don't work for a client that is unprofitable or is making you unhappy or uncomfortable—there's too much business out there for you to invest your time that way.

Financial Management

One of the primary indicators of the overall health of your business is its financial status, and it's important that you monitor your financial progress closely. The only way you can do that is to keep good records. You can handle the process manually or use any of the excellent computer accounting software programs on the market. You might want to ask your accountant for assistance getting your system of books set up. The key is to get set up and keep your records current and accurate throughout the life of your company.

Keeping good records helps generate financial statements that tell you exactly where you stand and what you need to do next. The key financial statements you need to understand and use regularly are:

- *Profit and loss statement (also called the P&L or income statement).* This illustrates how much your company is making or losing over a designated period— monthly, quarterly, or annually—by subtracting expenses from revenue to arrive at a net result, which is either a profit or a loss.

Profit and Loss Statement

ABC Business Support Service
January 200x–December 200x

Income

Sales	$85,950
Total Income	**$85,950**

Expenses

Bank service charges	$300
Dues and subscriptions	450
Insurance	1,000
Licenses and permits	75
Office supplies	1,025
Payroll	58,000
Professional fees	850
Rent	6,000
Telephone	1,200
Utilities	2,200
Total Expenses	**$71,100**
Net Income (Profit)	**$14,850**

- *Balance sheet.* A table showing your assets, liabilities, and capital at a specific point. A balance sheet is typically generated monthly, quarterly, or annually when the books are closed.
- *Cash flow statement.* Summarizes the operating, investing, and financing activities of your business as they relate to the inflow and outflow of cash. As with the profit and loss statement, a cash flow statement is prepared to reflect a specific accounting period, such as monthly, quarterly, or annually.

Successful business support service owners review these reports regularly, at least monthly, so they always know where they stand and can move quickly to correct minor difficulties before they become major financial problems. If you wait until November to figure out whether or not you made a profit in February, you won't be in business for long. But monitoring your financial progress takes discipline, particularly when you're growing fast and working hard. If you don't do it, warns an entrepreneur, you'll find yourself at the end of the year with nothing to show for your hard work, and not knowing how to improve your profitability the following year.

Setting Credit Policies

When you extend credit to someone, you are essentially providing them with an interest-free loan. You wouldn't expect someone to lend you money without getting information from you about where you live and work, and your ability to repay. It just makes sense that you would want to get this information from someone you are lending money to.

Reputable companies will not object to providing you with credit information, or even paying a deposit on large projects. If you don't feel comfortable asking for at least part of the money upfront, just think how uncomfortable you'll feel if you do the work and deliver a major project and don't get paid at all. You might feel awkward asking for a deposit or insisting on a complete credit application—until the first time you get burned. Then it will be easy.

Joann feels that "as long as they have a company name, address, and phone listing, I'll extend credit," she says. "If they come in off the street, I won't take a personal check; I insist on a company check."

Extending credit involves some risk, but the advantages of judiciously granted credit far outweigh the potential losses. Extending credit promotes customer loyalty. People will call you over a competitor because they already have an account set up and it's easy for them. Customers also often spend money more easily when they don't have to pay cash. Finally, if you ever decide to sell your business, it will have a greater value because you can show steady accounts.

Typically, you will only extend credit to businesses. Individuals will likely pay cash (or by check) at the time of purchase, or use a credit card. You need to decide how much risk you are willing to take by setting limits on how much credit you will allow each account. Also, it's a good idea to check the account status when accepting a project from a client on open credit. If the account is past due or the balance is unusually high, you may want to negotiate different terms before increasing the amount owed.

> ### Bright Idea
> Photocopy checks before depositing them. That way, if a collection problem occurs later, you have the client's current bank information in your files—that makes collecting on a judgment much easier.

Your credit policy should include a clear collection strategy. Do not ignore overdue bills; the older a bill gets, the less likely it will ever be paid. Be prepared to take action on past-due accounts as soon as they become past due.

Billing

If you're extending credit to your customers—and it's likely you will if your clients are businesses rather than individuals—you need to establish and follow sound billing procedures.

Taxing Matters

Businesses are required to pay a wide range of taxes, and business support services are no exception. Keep good records so you can offset your local, state, and federal income taxes with the expenses of operating your company. If you sell supplies, even in small quantities, you'll probably be required by your state to charge and collect sales tax. If you have employees, you'll be responsible for paying payroll taxes. If you operate as a corporation, you'll have to pay payroll taxes for yourself; as a sole proprietor, you'll pay self-employment tax. Then there are property taxes, taxes on your equipment and inventory, fees and taxes to maintain your corporate status, your business license fee (which is really a tax), and other lesser-known taxes. Take the time to review all of your tax liabilities with your accountant.

> **Beware!**
>
> Including fliers or brochures with your invoices is a great marketing tool, but remember that adding an insert may cause the envelope to require extra postage. Getting the marketing message out is probably worth the extra few cents in mailing costs; just be sure you check the total weight before you mail so your invoices aren't returned to you for insufficient postage—or worse, delivered "postage due."

Coordinate your billing system with your customers' payable procedures. Candidly ask what you can do to ensure prompt payment; that may include confirming the correct billing address and finding out what documentation is required to help the customer determine the validity of the invoice. Keep in mind that many large companies pay certain types of invoices on certain days of the month; find out if your customers do that, and schedule your invoices to arrive in time for the next payment cycle.

Most computer bookkeeping software programs include basic invoices. If you design your own invoices and statements, be sure they are clear and easy to understand. Detail each item, and indicate the amount due in bold with the words "Please pay" in front of the total. A confusing invoice may get set aside for clarification, and your payment will be delayed.

Most of the operators we talked with find it practical to issue an invoice as each project is completed and often include the invoice with the finished work. That's when customer appreciation is highest, and when they're thinking about you in a positive way, they're more likely to process your invoice quickly. If necessary, send out monthly statements summarizing what amounts are outstanding.

Finally, use your invoices as a marketing tool. Print notices of new services or reminders of services your clients may not be fully using on them. For example, after you list the items you are billing for, you might add a line that reads "We offer full mailing list management services; call us for details" or "Can't keep up with maintaining your Web page? Let us do it for you." You can also add a flier or brochure to the envelope—even though the invoice is going to an existing customer, you never know where your brochures will end up.

Checking It Twice

Just because a customer passed your first credit check with flying colors doesn't mean you should never re-evaluate their credit status—in fact, you should do it on a regular basis.

Tell customers when you initially grant their credit that you have a policy of periodically reviewing accounts so that when you do it, it's not a surprise. Remember, things can change very quickly in the business world, and a company that is on sound

▲

financial footing this year may be quite wobbly next year.

An annual re-evaluation of all customers on open account is a good idea—but if you start to see trouble in the interim, don't wait to take action. Another time to re-evaluate a customer's credit is when they request an increase in their credit line.

Some key trouble signs are a slow down in payments, unusual complaints about the quality of your work that you weren't getting before, and difficulty getting answers to your payment inquiries. Even a sharp increase in volume could signal trouble; companies concerned that they may lose their credit privileges may try to buy on credit while they can. Pay attention to what your customers are doing; a major change in their customer base or product line is something you may want to monitor.

Take the same approach to a credit review as you do to a new credit application. Most of the time, you can use what you have on file to conduct the check, but if you're concerned for any reason, you may want to ask the customer for updated information.

Most customers will understand routine credit reviews and accept them as a sound business practice. A customer who objects may well have something to hide—and that's something you need to know.

> **Bright Idea**
>
> Any of the popular off-the-shelf business bookkeeping and financial management software packages can help you maintain your financial records and handle billing and accounts payable.

Accepting Credit and Debit Cards

Accepting credit cards is not as common in the business support service industry as it is in other industries, such as retail and restaurants. Joann used to accept credit cards, but her clients weren't using the service, so she discontinued it. However, if your market includes a substantial number of individuals (resume clients, students, etc.) and even small businesses, your clients may appreciate being able to pay by credit card. It's much easier now to get merchant status than it has been in the past; in fact, these days merchant status providers are competing aggressively for your business.

To get a credit card merchant account, start with your own bank. Also check with various professional associations that offer merchant status as a member benefit. Shop around; this is a competitive industry, and it's worth taking the time to get the best deal.

Accepting Checks

Checks will likely be your most common form of payment. When you receive a check, look for several key items. Make sure the check is drawn on a local bank. Check the date for accuracy. Do not accept a check that is undated, postdated, or more than 30 days old. Be sure the written amount and numerical amount agree.

If you accept a check from an individual, ask to see identification so you can locate the customer in case you have a problem with the check. The most valid and valuable piece of identification is a driver's license. In most states, this will include the driver's picture, signature, and address. If the signature, address, and name agree with what is printed on the check, you are probably safe. If the information does not agree, ask which is accurate and record that information on the check.

Human Resources

Though the majority of business support services are one-person operations, you may want a larger company. Or your goal may be to stay small, but you may need extra help once in a while. The best case would be if you started your business and you saw the opportunity to expand. Whatever the

▲

case, it's a good idea for you to understand the human resources aspects of owning a business.

The first step in formulating a comprehensive human resources program is to decide exactly what you want someone to do. The job description doesn't have to be as formal as one you might expect from a large corporation, but it needs to clearly outline the person's duties and responsibilities. It should also list any special skills or other required credentials, such as typing speed and software knowledge, or a valid driver's license and clean driving record for someone who is going to do deliveries for you.

Next, you need to establish a pay scale. Ranges vary by parts of the country and skill level required. An entrepreneur in California said they pay $11 to $14 per hour for employees whose primary responsibility is word processing. Bill Pypes says the highest rate he's paid in Iowa is $9 per hour (at the time of the interview), and the lowest is minimum wage (to an employee who wasn't a particularly fast typist but who was accurate and reliable). You can get a good idea of the pay ranges in your area simply by checking the classified ads in your local paper or online job posting site.

You'll also need a job application form. You can get a basic form at most office supply stores, or you can create your own. In any case, have your attorney review the form you'll be using for compliance with the most current employment laws. There is a sample employment application that you can tailor to your needs on page 143.

Every prospective employee should fill out an application—even if it's someone you know, and even if they have submitted a detailed resume. A resume is not a signed, sworn statement acknowledging that you can fire them if they lie; an application is. The application will also help you verify their resume; compare the two and make sure the information is consistent.

Now you're ready to start looking for candidates.

Looking in the Right Places

Picture the ideal candidate in your mind. Is this person likely to be unemployed and reading the classified ads? It is possible, but you will probably improve your chances for a successful hire if you are more creative in your search techniques than simply writing a "help wanted" ad.

Sources for prospective employees include suppliers, former co-workers, customers, and professional associations. Check with nearby colleges and perhaps even high schools for part-time help. Put the word out among your social contacts as well—you never know who might know the perfect person for your operation. Joann Voss agrees that it's hard to find good assistance; she says word-of-mouth works best for her as a recruiting tool, particularly with homebased independent contractors.

Employment Application

Your Company Name and Logo Here
Employment Application

Applicant Information

Name: _____

Company: _____

Street address: _____

City: _____ State: _____ Zip: _____

Phone number: _____ Fax number: _____

E-mail address: _____

Position desired: _____ Date available: _____

WPM rate*: _____ (*Required for typing and transcription positions.)

Please list your software proficiencies: _____

_____

Are you a U.S. Citizen? _____

If no, are you authorized to work in the U.S.? _____

Have you ever been convicted of a felony? _____

If yes, please explain: _____

_____

Education

High school: _____ City/state: _____

Dates attended: _____ to _____ Did you graduate? _____

College/university: _____ City/state: _____

Dates attended: _____ to _____ Did you graduate? _____

Degree(s) achieved: _____

Employment Application, continued

Other education: _____ City/state: _____

Dates attended: _____ to _____ Did you graduate? _____

Degrees/certifications achieved: _____

_____

References

Please list at least three personal or professional references.

Full name: _____ Relationship/company: _____

E-mail address: _____ Phone: _____

Full name: _____ Relationship/company: _____

E-mail address: _____ Phone: _____

Full name: _____ Relationship/company: _____

E-mail address: _____ Phone: _____

Employment History

Company 1: _____

Address: _____

Position held: _____

Starting wages: _____ Ending wages: _____

From: _____ to _____

Reason for leaving: _____

Previous supervisor: _____ May we contact for reference? _____

Company 2: _____

Address: _____

Position held: _____

Starting wages: _____ Ending wages: _____

Employment Application, continued

From: _____ to _____

Reason for leaving: _____

Previous supervisor: _____ May we contact for reference? _____

Company 3: _____

Address: _____

Position held: _____

Starting wages: _____ Ending wages: _____

From: _____ to _____

Reason for leaving: _____

Previous supervisor: _____ May we contact for reference? _____

Disclaimer and Signature:

I certify that my answers are true and complete to the best of my knowledge.

If this applications leads to employment, I understand that false or misleading information in my application or interview may result in my release.

Signature: _____ Date: _____

Use caution if you decide to hire friends and relatives—many personal relationships are not strong enough to survive an employee-employer situation. Small-business owners in all industries tell of nightmarish experiences when a friend or relative refused to accept direction or in other ways abused a personal relationship in the course of business.

The key to success as an employer is making it clear from the start that you are the one in charge. You don't need to act like a dictator, of course. Be diplomatic, but set the ground rules in advance and stick to them.

▲

```
┌─────────────────────────────────────────────────────────────┐
│                      Job Description                          │
├─────────────────────────────────────────────────────────────┤
```

Position: Typist/Transcriptionist

Duties: Word processing and transcription; occasionally answer telephone and greet clients; interact with clients as necessary to clarify and complete work.

Required skills: Minimum typing speed of 70 words per minute; proficient in Microsoft Word; able to operate transcription machine; knowledge of punctuation and grammar; and the ability to proofread.

Evaluating Applicants

When you actually begin the hiring process, don't be surprised if you're as nervous at the prospect of interviewing potential employees as they are about being interviewed. After all, they may need a job—but the future of your company is at stake.

It's a good idea to prepare your interview questions in advance. Develop open-ended questions that encourage the candidate to talk. In addition to knowing what they've done, you want to find out how they did it. Ask each candidate for a particular position on the same set of questions, and take notes as they respond so you can make an accurate assessment and comparison later.

You also need to evaluate their skills. Have them take a standard typing test to measure their speed. How fast you will require them to type is a judgment call you must make, and it will be based in great part on the particular work they'll be doing. For example, someone who will spend most of their time doing desktop publishing and page layout doesn't need to be a fast typist, but speed and accuracy is critical for a transcriptionist.

Joann insists on a minimum typing speed of 75 words per minute for her transcriptionists even though she pays by the page. She says, "When you get paid by the page, if you're

Tip...

Smart Tip
A great place to look for part-time employees or independent contractors is among full-time secretarial/administrative professionals who might want to do some work on the side to earn extra money. These workers are most likely to be available at night and on weekends, which lets you expand the scope and speed of your services. Find them by networking among people you know and putting the word out through local professional associations.

under that, you don't make enough money for yourself. If you're at 75 words per minute, you're going to make approximately $12 an hour. A lot of my transcriptionists are at 90 words per minute and above, so they make about $15 an hour."

You should also administer a test to assess candidates' grammar and punctuation skills. You can either make up your own test or purchase tests through commercial testing firms or human resources consultants.

You'll also want to confirm each candidate's familiarity with the software you use. In most cases, it won't be essential that they know your programs; if they have basic computer skills, it shouldn't take them long to learn new same-purpose software.

You probably won't want to invest the time and money in training a new hire on more complex programs such as ones that do spreadsheets or desktop publishing. Insist that candidates who are going to be working on these types of programs demonstrate their proficiency. Get them to talk about the software, ask them to show you projects they've completed using those programs, and give them a small project they can do as a test.

Don't accept what candidates put on their resumes or applications at face value; interview and test to be sure they have the skill level necessary to produce the quality of work you want for your clients.

When the interview is over, let the candidate know what to expect. Is it going to take you several weeks to interview other candidates, check references, and make a decision? Will you want the top candidates to return for a second interview? Will you call the candidate, or should they call you? This is not only a good business practice; it's also just simple common courtesy.

Always check former employers and personal references. Though many companies are very restrictive as to what information they'll verify, you may be surprised at what you can find out. Certainly you should at least confirm that the applicant told the truth about dates and positions held. Personal references are likely to give you some additional insight into the general character and personality of the candidate; this will help you decide if they'll fit into your operation.

Keep in mind that under the Immigration Reform and Control Act of 1986, you may only hire persons who may legally work in the United States, which means citizens and nationals of the United States, and aliens authorized to work in the United States. As an employer, you must verify the identity and employment eligibility of everyone you hire.

> **Beware!**
> Be honest with candidates about the work they're going to be doing. Don't mislead them and insist that they'll be working on exciting, challenging projects if in reality they'll spend most of their time typing materials they find boring. Of course, if the work is truly interesting—as is much of the transcribing Joann's company does—use that fact as a recruiting tool.

Who's Who?

Some of the projects you'll do will require little more than strong typing skills and an awareness of spelling and grammar; other projects will require some very specific expertise. Also, as your company grows, you'll want to consider hiring people to handle management and marketing for your firm. Here is a sample of the workers you may need:

○ *Typist/word processor*. This is the foundation of your staff, the person who does the bulk of the work by typing documents, transcribing tapes, and doing other data entry work.

○ *Secretary/administrative assistant*. For both yourself and your clients, this individual types and handles other administrative chores.

○ *Receptionist/telephone operator*. This person will greet visitors, direct calls, and take messages for your business as well as for your clients if you're in an executive suite situation or if you offer telephone answering as part of your service package.

○ *Graphic designer*. This is the creative person who does page layout and design for your clients' brochures, newsletters, presentations, and other materials.

○ *Editor/proofreader*. Checking copy for accuracy and clarity is this person's critical function and special talent.

○ *Office manager*. As your business grows, you may want to turn the day-to-day running of the office over to a manager.

○ *Supervisor*. Depending on the size of your staff, you may need one or more supervisors or team leaders to adequately direct and supervise the workload.

○ *Sales/marketing rep*. As the business owner, you'll do the majority of sales and marketing, especially in the beginning. However, as your company grows, you may want to hire someone to generate new business on a part-time or full-time basis.

During the interviewing process, let the applicant know that you'll be doing this. Once you have made the job offer and the person is brought on board, you must complete the Employment Eligibility Verification Form (I–9) and then retain it for at least three years, or one year after employment ends, whichever period of time is longer.

Be sure to document every step of the interview and reference-checking process. Even very small companies are finding themselves targets of employment discrimination suits;

if it happens to you, good records are your best defense.

When you are bringing an employee on board, it's important to protect yourself since you are opening your business to them. Below is a sample of a non-compete agreement to tailor to your needs to ensure that the information from your office isn't being shared nor can your employee use the experience with you to become a direct competitor.

Smart Tip

Training employees—even part-time, temporary help—in your way of doing things is important. They represent your company and need to know how to maintain the image and standards you've worked hard to establish.

Example 1

This example is a complete agreement that you can fill in and use for an employee who does not have a separate written employment contract.

Non-Disclosure and Non-Competition. (a) At all times while this agreement is in force and after its expiration or termination, [employee name] agrees to refrain from disclosing [company name]'s customer lists, trade secrets, or other confidential material. [Employee name] agrees to take reasonable security measures to prevent accidental disclosure and industrial espionage.

(b) While this agreement is in force, the employee agrees to use [his/her] best efforts to [describe job] and to abide by the nondisclosure and non-competition terms of this agreement; the employer agrees to compensate the employee as follows: [describe compensation]. After expiration or termination of this agreement, [employee name] agrees not to compete with [company name] for a period of [number] years within a [number] mile radius of [company name and location]. This prohibition will not apply if this agreement is terminated because [company] violated the terms of this agreement.

Competition means owning or working for a business of the following type: [specify type of business employee may not engage in]

(c) [Employee name] agrees to pay liquidated damages in the amount of $[dollar amount] for any violation of the covenant not to compete contained in subparagraph (b) of this paragraph.

IN WITNESS WHEREOF, [company name] and [employee name] have signed this agreement.

_____

[company name]

_____

[employee's name]

Date: _____

▲

Example 2

This example is part of a larger agreement, such as an employment contract or an employee handbook. You can use it as a separate agreement or incorporate it into another, larger document.

Non-Disclosure and Non-Competition. (a) After expiration or termination of this agreement, [employee name] agrees to respect the confidentiality of [company name] patents, trademarks, and trade secrets, and not to disclose them to anyone.

(b) [Employee name] agrees not to make use of research done in the course of work done for [company name] while employed by a competitor of [company name]

(c) [Employee name] agrees not to set up in business as a direct competitor of [company name] within a radius of [number] miles of [company name and location] for a period of [number and measure of time (e.g., "four months" or "10 years")] following the expiration or termination of this agreement.

(d) [Employee name] agrees to pay liquidated damages of $[dollar amount] if any violation of this paragraph is proved or admitted.

IN WITNESS WHEREOF, [company name] and [employee name] have signed this agreement.

_____

[company name]

_____

[employee's name]

Date: _____

Once They're on Board

The hiring process is only the beginning of the challenge of having employees. The next thing you need to do is train them.

Many small businesses conduct their "training" just by throwing someone into the job, but that's not fair to the employee, and it's certainly not good for your business. If you think you can't afford to spend time on training, think again—can you afford not to adequately train your employees? Do you want your employees working on projects or interacting with your clients when you haven't told them how you want things done?

In an ideal world, employees could be hired already knowing everything they need to know. But this isn't an ideal world, and if you want the job done right, you have to teach your people how to do it.

Whether done in a formal classroom setting or on the job, effective training begins with a clear goal and a plan for reaching it. Training falls into one of three categories: orientation, which includes explaining company policies and procedures; job skills, which focuses on how to do specific tasks; and ongoing development, which enhances basic job skills and grooms employees for future challenges and opportunities. These tips will help you maximize your training efforts:

- *Find out how people learn best.* Delivering training is not a one-size-fits-all proposition. People absorb and process information differently, and your training method needs to be compatible with their individual preferences. Some people can read a manual, others prefer a verbal explanation, and still others need to see a demonstration.

- *Be a strong role model.* Don't expect more from your employees than you are willing to do. You're a good role model when you do things the way they should be done all the time. Don't take shortcuts you don't want your employees to take or behave in any way you don't want them to behave. On the other hand, don't assume that simply doing things the right way is enough to teach others how to do things. Role-modeling is not a substitute for training; it reinforces training. If you only role-model but never train, employees aren't likely to get the message.

- *Look for training opportunities.* Once you get beyond basic orientation and job skills training, you need to constantly be on the lookout for opportunities to enhance the skill and performance levels of your people.

- *Make it real.* Whenever possible, use real-life situations to train—but avoid letting clients know they've become a training experience for employees.

- *Anticipate questions.* Don't assume that employees know what to ask. In a new situation, people often don't understand enough to formulate questions. Anticipate their questions and answer them in advance.

- *Ask for feedback.* Finally, encourage your employees to let you know how you are doing as a trainer. Just as you evaluate their performance, convince them that it's OK to tell you the truth, ask your employees what they thought of the training and your techniques, and use that information to improve your own training skills.

Employee Benefits

The actual wages you pay may be only part of your employees' total compensation. While many very small companies do not offer a formal benefits program, more and more business owners have recognized that benefits—particularly in the area of insurance—are extremely important when it comes to attracting and retaining quality employees. In most parts of the country, the employment rate is higher than it's been in decades, which means competition for good people is stiff.

The law requires employers to provide employees with certain benefits that are not optional:

- Give employees time off to vote, serve on a jury, and perform military service.
- Comply with all workers' compensation requirements.
- Withhold FICA taxes from employees' paychecks and pay your portion of FICA taxes, providing employees with retirement and disability benefits.
- Pay state and federal unemployment taxes.
- Contribute to state short-term disability programs where they exist.
- Comply with the Federal Family and Medical Leave Act.

Typical benefits packages include group insurance (your employees may pay all or a portion of their premiums), paid holidays, and vacations. Some services offer year-end bonuses based on the company's profitability. You can build employee loyalty by seeking additional benefits that may be somewhat unusual—and they don't have to cost much. For example, if you're in a retail location, talk to other store owners in your shopping center to see if they're interested in providing reciprocal employee discounts. You'll not only provide your own employees with a benefit, but you may get some new customers out of the arrangement.

Some other employee perks could be low or no-cost ideas like these:

- *Work-from-home days.* If you have your employees work from a commercial office, set them up to work at home a few days a week.
- *Community service days.* Give your employees a few paid days each year to take part in community or charitable activities that they may not have time for otherwise.
- *Pizza Fridays.* Bring pizza or sandwiches into the office every Friday. It doesn't matter what you bring but make sure to treat to whole office. A couple pizzas might only cost you $20 or so.
- *Movie tickets.* Another $20 idea is to offer a pair of movie passes to an employee each month. This may be a way of rewarding a star employee or just as a morale booster.
- *Free car washes.* A basic car wash costs about $5 each, so offer a free car wash to your employees every once in a while. It's

Smart Tip

No matter how much you enjoy your work, you need an occasional break from it, whether it's to take a vacation or to deal with an illness or personal emergency. Be sure your employees and subcontractors are well-trained and committed to maintaining your service levels whether you are there or not.

not the money you put in but the thought and the reward of giving them a shiny clean car to use for the rest of the week.

- *Barter days*. If your services allow you to swap services with another company, do so and pass the benefits on to your employees, such as doing a brochure for a local coffee shop and getting free coffee coupons in return.

- *Continental breakfasts*. It may not be a free lunch, but a free breakfast every once in a while always brightens a morning. Think of alternating it with other perks so it doesn't become an expectation and fixed cost.

> **Bright Idea**
>
> If you have employees, consider using a payroll service rather than trying to handle this task yourself. The service will calculate taxes; handle reporting and paying local, state, and federal payroll taxes; make deductions for savings, insurance premiums, loan payments, etc.; and may offer other benefits to you and your employees.

- *Holiday parties*. You may not have a big office or a large staff, but celebrate the holidays and throw a party anyway. Celebrate with your staff and their families and see the morale boost through the new year.

One type of insurance may not be optional. In most states, if you have three or more employees, you are required by law to carry workers' compensation insurance. This coverage pays medical expenses and replaces a portion of the employee's wages if he or she is injured on the job. Although the chances of such an injury are low in this industry, even if you have only one or two employees, you may want to consider this coverage to protect both them and you in the event of an accident, or if they develop any physical problems related to repetitive motion, such as carpal tunnel syndrome from typing.

Details and requirements vary by state; contact your state's insurance office or your own insurance agent for information so you can be sure to be in compliance.

Beyond tangible benefits, look for ways to provide positive working conditions. Consider flexible working hours, establish family-friendly policies, and be sure the physical environment is comfortable and designed to enhance productivity.

Independent Contractors

The business support service industry is very conducive to working with independent contractors, either on an hourly or per-project basis. From an administrative perspective, independent contractors are much easier to deal with than employees—you simply pay them for the work they do, and they're responsible for their own taxes, benefits, etc.

It's important to build a relationship with your independent contractors, just as you would with employees. Although they will typically work from home, get to know them and make them feel like a valued member of your team.

It's also a good idea to have them sign an agreement that defines your relationship, confirms their independent contractor status, establishes work standards, and addresses confidentiality and competitive issues. For example, Joann of Voss Transcriptions' agreement requires typists to delete any client data from their computers within 30 days of completing the project and prevents them from discussing client work with anyone outside the firm. You'll also want to prohibit independent contractors from by-passing you and going directly to your clients to get the work.

Joann has transcriptionists who have worked for her as independent contractors for as long as ten years. "They pick and choose the projects and how much they want to work," she says. "I have some who make $250 every two weeks and some who make $2,000. It's totally up to them."

It's also important to be sure your independent contractors meet the requirements set by the IRS.

Take a look at the sample Independent Contractor Agreement from SmartBiz.com on page 155 that they designed to help draft a custom agreement that fits your needs.

Independent Contractor Agreement

This Agreement is entered into as of the [   ] day of [   ], 20[   ], between [company name] ("the Company") and [service provider's name] ("the Contractor").

Independent Contractor. Subject to the terms and conditions of this Agreement, the Company hereby engages the Contractor as an independent contractor to perform the services set forth herein, and the Contractor hereby accepts such engagement.

Duties, Term, and Compensation. The Contractor's duties, term of engagement, compensation and provisions for payment thereof shall be as set forth in the estimate previously provided to the Company by the Contractor and which is attached as Exhibit A, which may be amended in writing from time to time, or supplemented with subsequent estimates for services to be rendered by the Contractor and agreed to by the Company, and which collectively are hereby incorporated by reference.

Expenses. During the term of this Agreement, the Contractor shall bill and the Company shall reimburse [him or her] for all reasonable and approved out-of-pocket expenses which are incurred in connection with the performance of the duties hereunder. Notwithstanding the foregoing, expenses for the time spend by Consultant in traveling to and from Company facilities shall not be reimbursable.

Written Reports. The Company may request that project plans, progress reports and a final results report be provided by Consultant on a monthly basis. A final results report shall be due at the conclusion of the project and shall be submitted to the Company in a confidential written report at such time. The results report shall be in such form and setting forth such information and data as is reasonably requested by the Company.

Inventions. Any and all inventions, discoveries, developments and innovations conceived by the Contractor during this engagement relative to the duties under this Agreement shall be the exclusive property of the Company; and the Contractor hereby assigns all right, title, and interest in the same to the Company. Any and all inventions, discoveries, developments and innovations conceived by the Contractor prior to the term of this Agreement and utilized by [him or her] in rendering duties to the Company are hereby licensed to the Company for use in its operations and for an infinite duration. This license is non-exclusive, and may be assigned without the Contractor's prior written approval by the Company to a wholly-owned subsidiary of the Company.

Confidentiality. The Contractor acknowledges that during the engagement [he or she] will have access to and become acquainted with various trade secrets, inventions, innovations, processes, information, records and specifications owned or licensed by the Company and/or used by the Company in connection with the operation of its

Independent Contractor Agreement, continued

business including, without limitation, the Company's business and product processes, methods, customer lists, accounts and procedures. The Contractor agrees that [he or she] will not disclose any of the aforesaid, directly or indirectly, or use any of them in any manner, either during the term of this Agreement or at any time thereafter, except as required in the course of this engagement with the Company. All files, records, documents, blueprints, specifications, information, letters, notes, media lists, original artwork/creative, notebooks, and similar items relating to the business of the Company, whether prepared by the Contractor or otherwise coming into [his or her] possession, shall remain the exclusive property of the Company. The Contractor shall not retain any copies of the foregoing without the Company's prior written permission. Upon the expiration or earlier termination of this Agreement, or whenever requested by the Company, the Contractor shall immediately deliver to the Company all such files, records, documents, specifications, information, and other items in [his or her] possession or under [his or her] control. The Contractor further agrees that [he or she] will not disclose [his or her] retention as an independent contractor or the terms of this Agreement to any person without the prior written consent of the Company and shall at all times preserve the confidential nature of [his or her] relationship to the Company and of the services hereunder.

Conflicts of Interest; Non-hire Provision. The Contractor represents that [he or she] is free to enter into this Agreement, and that this engagement does not violate the terms of any agreement between the Contractor and any third party. Further, the Contractor, in rendering [his or her] duties shall not utilize any invention, discovery, development, improvement, innovation, or trade secret in which [he or she] does not have a proprietary interest. During the term of this agreement, the Contractor shall devote as much of [his or her] productive time, energy and abilities to the performance of [his or her] duties hereunder as is necessary to perform the required duties in a timely and productive manner. The Contractor is expressly free to perform services for other parties while performing services for the Company. For a period of six months following any termination, the Contractor shall not, directly or indirectly hire, solicit, or encourage to leave the Company's employment, any employee, consultant, or contractor of the Company or hire any such employee, consultant, or contractor who has left the Company's employment or contractual engagement within one year of such employment or engagement.

Right to Injunction. The parties hereto acknowledge that the services to be rendered by the Contractor under this Agreement and the rights and privileges granted to the Company under the Agreement are of a special, unique, unusual, and extraordinary character which gives them a peculiar value, the loss of which cannot be reasonably or adequately compensated by damages in any action at law, and the breach by the

Contractor of any of the provisions of this Agreement will cause the Company irreparable injury and damage. The Contractor expressly agrees that the Company shall be entitled to injunctive and other equitable relief in the event of, or to prevent, a breach of any provision of this Agreement by the Contractor. Resort to such equitable relief, however, shall not be construed to be a waiver of any other rights or remedies that the Company may have for damages or otherwise. The various rights and remedies of the Company under this Agreement or otherwise shall be construed to be cumulative, and no one of the them shall be exclusive of any other or of any right or remedy allowed by law.

Merger. This Agreement shall not be terminated by the merger or consolidation of the Company into or with any other entity.

Termination. The Company may terminate this Agreement at any time by 10 working days' written notice to the Contractor. In addition, if the Contractor is convicted of any crime or offense, fails or refuses to comply with the written policies or reasonable directive of the Company, is guilty of serious misconduct in connection with performance hereunder, or materially breaches provisions of this Agreement, the Company at any time may terminate the engagement of the Contractor immediately and without prior written notice to the Contractor.

Independent Contractor. This Agreement shall not render the Contractor an employee, partner, agent of, or joint venturer with the Company for any purpose. The Contractor is and will remain an independent contractor in [his or her] relationship to the Company. The Company shall not be responsible for withholding taxes with respect to the Contractor's compensation hereunder. The Contractor shall have no claim against the Company hereunder or otherwise for vacation pay, sick leave, retirement benefits, social security, worker's compensation, health or disability benefits, unemployment insurance benefits, or employee benefits of any kind.

Insurance. The Contractor will carry liability insurance (including malpractice insurance, if warranted) relative to any service that [he or she] performs for the Company.

Successors and Assigns. All of the provisions of this Agreement shall be binding upon and inure to the benefit of the parties hereto and their respective heirs, if any, successors, and assigns.

Choice of Law. The laws of the state of [ ] shall govern the validity of this Agreement, the construction of its terms and the interpretation of the rights and duties of the parties hereto.

Arbitration. Any controversies arising out of the terms of this Agreement or its interpretation shall be settled in [ ] in accordance with the rules of the American

Independent Contractor Agreement, continued

Arbitration Association, and the judgment upon award may be entered in any court having jurisdiction thereof.

Headings. Section headings are not to be considered a part of this Agreement and are not intended to be a full and accurate description of the contents hereof.

Waiver. Waiver by one party hereto of breach of any provision of this Agreement by the other shall not operate or be construed as a continuing waiver.

Assignment. The Contractor shall not assign any of [his or her] rights under this Agreement, or delegate the performance of any of [his or her] duties hereunder, without the prior written consent of the Company.

Notices. Any and all notices, demands, or other communications required or desired to be given hereunder by any party shall be in writing and shall be validly given or made to another party if personally served, or if deposited in the United States mail, certified or registered, postage prepaid, return receipt requested. If such notice or demand is served personally, notice shall be deemed constructively made at the time of such personal service. If such notice, demand or other communication is given by mail, such notice shall be conclusively deemed given five days after deposit thereof in the United States mail addressed to the party to whom such notice, demand or other communication is to be given as follows:

If to the Contractor: [name]
                                   [street address]
                                   [city, state, zip]

If to the Company: [name]
                                   [street address]
                                   [city, state, zip]

Any party hereto may change its address for purposes of this paragraph by written notice given in the manner provided above.

Modification or Amendment. No amendment, change or modification of this Agreement shall be valid unless in writing signed by the parties hereto.

Entire Understanding. This document and any exhibit attached constitute the entire understanding and agreement of the parties, and any and all prior agreements, understandings, and representations are hereby terminated and canceled in their entirety and are of no further force and effect.

Unenforceability of Provisions. If any provision of this Agreement, or any portion thereof, is held to be invalid and unenforceable, then the remainder of this Agreement shall nevertheless remain in full force and effect.

IN WITNESS WHEREOF the undersigned have executed this Agreement as of the day and year first written above. The parties hereto agree that facsimile signatures shall be as effective as if originals.

[company name]   [contractor's name]

By:_____   By:_____

Its: [title or position]   Its: [title or position]

SCHEDULE A

DUTIES, TERM, AND COMPENSATION

DUTIES: The Contractor will [describe here the work or service to be performed]. [He or she] will report directly to [name] and to any other party designated by [name] in connection with the performance of the duties under this Agreement and shall fulfill any other duties reasonably requested by the Company and agreed to by the Contractor.

TERM: This engagement shall commence upon execution of this Agreement and shall continue in full force and effect through [date] or earlier upon completion of the Contractor's duties under this Agreement. The Agreement may only be extended thereafter by mutual agreement, unless terminated earlier by operation of and in accordance with this Agreement.

COMPENSATION: (Choose A or B)

A. As full compensation for the services rendered pursuant to this Agreement, the Company shall pay the Contractor at the hourly rate of [dollar amount] per hour, with total payment not to exceed [dollar amount] without prior written approval by an authorized representative of the Company. Such compensation shall be payable within 30 days of receipt of Contractor's monthly invoice for services rendered supported by reasonable documentation.

B. As full compensation for the services rendered pursuant to this Agreement, the Company shall pay the Contractor the sum of [dollar amount], to be paid [time and conditions of payment.]

Tales from the
Trenches

By now, you should know how to get started
and have a good idea of what to do—and not do—in your own
business support service. But nothing teaches as well as the
voice of experience. So we asked established operators to tell
us what has contributed to their success; here's what they had
to say.

Bypassing Common Mistakes

Stat Fact
Of the 40 surveyed entrepreneurs, 40 percent have been in business for five years or more and 25 percent have been running for three to five years. There are great success rates for this industry.

Although success comes from trial and error, we want to make sure you are well-prepared to succeed. Here are some of the most common mistakes our business owners experienced:

- Inability to complete the simple exercise of identifying your best product or service, unique selling proposition (USP), and ideal client.
- Failure to clarify direction (breaking your niche down to its smallest segment).
- Refusing to develop short- and long-term goals.
- Failing to create a cohesive marketing strategy and sticking to it, in good and lean times.
- Not participating in mentoring, coaching, or training programs that will enhance skills and increase marketability.
- Not joining industry organizations sooner since they offer a wealth of information and support.
- Not learning sooner how to say "no" and to keep from overextending myself.
- Not defining my target niche within my first year planning process.
- Spending money too quickly. (Keep your business plan and budget updated!)

Tell Everyone About What You Do

Never miss an opportunity to tell people about what you do for a living. You never know where you will meet that next client. One of Charlene Davis' best clients came from a casual conversation, during which she mentioned that she had started a word-processing service. "That person called me a few weeks later and asked if I could do some transcribing," Charlene recalls. "Later, she told me she probably wouldn't have outsourced the work to a stranger, but since she felt like she knew me, although not very well, she felt comfortable calling me. She has become a steady client, and she regularly refers other clients to me—all from one short conversation."

Sharon Williams, of the Alliance for Virtual Businesses and The 24 Hour Secretary, tells that "during the early portion of my business, I spent countless days networking and associating with successful business owners. These individuals were my mentors and essentially my unofficial advisory board, providing advice and assistance when requested. Their support strengthened my resolve and was a tremendous influence in the growth and direction of my business."

Thrive Under Pressure

In this business, it's just one deadline after another, operators report. When one project is done, the next one is waiting, and you don't get much of a break in between. "This is a service business that involves deadlines for almost every customer," says Bill Pypes. "Once in a while, there is somebody who says 'Call me back in a month or two when you're done,' but usually they want it yesterday. You need to be able to work well under deadline pressure."

Keep Plenty of Supplies on Hand

Always have a good stock of supplies on hand—paper, toner, ink cartridges, labels, etc.—so you don't run out in the middle of a project. "You will run out of toner or ink at the most unexpected and inconvenient time," says Charlene. "I learned the hard way. Once I ran out of ink in the middle of the night. Another time, I was planning to work late in the evening preparing a mailing that needed to go to the post office first thing the next morning. I thought I had more labels on hand than I did, and I ran out in the middle of the print run. I had to wait until the office supply store opened the next morning, and then finish printing the labels and preparing the mailing. I made it to the post office by the end of the day, but it was close, and it was later than the client would have preferred."

Even if you don't routinely work at night, Charlene adds, an unscheduled run to the office supply store is a serious time-waster and can affect the quality of service you give your clients. Set up a system to make sure your supplies never drop below a specific minimum level that is appropriate for your operation.

Raise Your Rates

If you're working too much but can't afford to cut back because you need the money, raise your rates. Sure, you'll probably lose a few clients, but they are the ones for whom price is more important than quality. Reasonable clients expect periodic rate increases.

> "My biggest mistake was sometimes not charging enough or believing in myself to charge the amount of money I am worth."
>
> —Gay Lynn Kirsch, Executive Secretarial Services, LLC

Stand Up for Yourself

Charlene says one of her biggest challenges has been dealing with clients who are very demanding. "One of my former clients was a nonprofit group. Their staff people were extremely demanding. When I began working for them, I explained that I was only working part time from home because I had a small baby. I told them I would do a good job at reasonable rates but that my family came first—that's what I tell all my clients, and that's how I run my business. But these people just didn't seem to grasp that. They'd call and want me to drop what I was doing, run over to their office and just do things in a rush without any regard to anything else I had to do," she says. "I talked with them about my policies over and over, and they would apologize and be thoughtful for a while; then they'd get back into these same last-minute, inconsiderate patterns. I finally told them that they needed someone who didn't mind working that way, and that I couldn't work for them anymore."

Although she felt the only solution with that client was to end their relationship, she says you can stand up for your rights and still preserve the client relationship in most cases. "I set reasonable boundaries, and I'm upfront and honest with my clients from the very beginning," she says. "Most of the time, they can live with that. And if they can't, I don't need their business."

Expect the Unexpected

No matter how long you're in the business or how many times you think you've seen it all, there will always be something to surprise you—an off-the-wall client, a bizarre project, an erratic employee—and you might as well get used to it.

Recognize the Value of Your Clients

Once you get a client on board, it is far more efficient and profitable to keep them than to lose them and find another one. "Make sure you treat customers right," advises Bill. "A good customer is hard to find. I've had one or two regular customers that I screwed up and lost, and you just want to kick yourself in the teeth when that happens."

> "Experience is the best teacher; get your feet wet working in the 'real world' building up contacts and capital before you try it on your own. Study everything you can get your hands on about starting up a business, setting up financing, developing a business plan, setting goals, marketing strategies, and developing your web site."
>
> —Sherry Watkins, Go2REassistant

Keep Your Employees and Independent Contractors Happy

Good workers are valuable, and trend-watchers say the employment situation isn't going to change any time soon. If you find someone who produces fast, accurate work, look for ways to build loyalty so you'll retain them. Treat workers fairly and with respect; don't allow clients to abuse them, and pay them as well as you can.

Joann says providing variety in their work also helps. "If they feel like they're in a rut and I can't offer them something else to work on, they'll leave. If I get someone working strictly on one contract, they're good for about six months, and then they're gone."

Get the Contract Signed
Before You Spend Any Money

Though it may not happen often, there may be times when you'll need to make special purchases (such as equipment, software, or supplies) to handle a particular project for a client. Before you invest in a project, be sure you will get the work. If a project requires an investment in training, staffing, or equipment, it's not unreasonable to insist on a contract and even an advance payment before you begin the work.

Final Words of Wisdom

There is so much opportunity out there if you are ready to sharpen your skills and sell them as an expert set of services. Our business owners had a few quick words of wisdom to those looking to start a business:

- Get a mentor and ask a lot of questions.
- Believe in yourself and block out the neigh-sayers.
- Network, network, network! You want to get to know people who can help build your business.
- Stay focused, pick a specialty and do it well.
- Keep up with and stay current with what's new.
- Volunteer and stay balanced.
- Do what you love to do and work with the people you want to work with. Your business then thrives because you are having fun.
- Realize that it's ok to change your focus. Go with what you're passionate about.
- Don't go in with guns blazing. Baby steps. If you can afford to, perhaps start part-time or do it on the side as casual work and see how it goes.
- Be patient and work hard. It doesn't happen overnight.
- Know your strengths and your weaknesses.

Joann says you need to be prepared, and that by doing so, "things have a tendency to work themselves out." She attributes her growth primarily to common sense. "It wasn't a lot of research or a lot of anything except hard work and common sense," she says. "I believe that if you work hard at anything and hang in there, your time will come. Be diligent and stick with it."

Appendix A
Business Support Resources

They say you can never be rich enough or young enough. While these could be argued, we believe you can never have enough resources. Therefore, we present for your consideration a wealth of sources for you to check into, check out, and harness for your own personal information blitz.

These sources are tidbits, ideas to get you started on your research. They are by no means the only sources out there and they should not be taken as the ultimate answer. We have done our research, but businesses do tend to move, change, fold, and expand. As we have repeatedly stressed, do your homework. Get out and start investigating.

Associations

Alliance for Virtual Businesses™, 8908 Liberty Road, Randallstown, MD 21133, (410) 521-7001, email: info@allianceforvirtualbiz.com, www.allianceforvirtualbiz.com

American Advertising Federation, 1101 Vermont Ave. NW, #500, Washington, DC 20004, (202) 898-0089, fax: (202) 898-0159, email: aaf@aaf.org, www.aaf.org

▲

American Accounting Association, 5717 Bessie Drive, Sarasota, FL 34233, (941) 921-7747, www.aaa-edu.org

American Home Business Association, 17 Harkim Rd, Greenwich, CT 06831, (203) 531-8552, www.homebusiness.com

American Institute of Certified Public Accountants, 1211 Ave. of the Americas, New York, NY 10036, (212) 596-6200, fax: (212) 596-6213, www.aicpa.org

American Management Association, 1601 Broadway, New York, NY 10019, (800) 262-9699, fax: (212) 903-8168, www.amanet.org

American Marketing Association, 211 S. Wacker Drive, #5800, Chicago, IL 60606, (800) AMA-1150, (312) 542-9000, fax: (312) 542-9001, e-mail: info@ama.org, www.ama.org

American Staffing Association, 277 S. Washington Street, #200, Alexandria, VA 22314, (703) 253-2020, fax: (703) 253-2053, asa@americanstaffing.net, www.american staffing.net

Association of Credit and Collection Professionals, P.O. Box 390106, Minneapolis, MN 55439, (952) 926-6547, www.ica-credit.org

Association of Small Business Development Centers, 8990 Burke Lake Road, Burke, VA 22015, (703) 764-9850, fax: (703) 764-1234, e-mail: info@asbdc-us.org, www.asbdc-us.org

Direct Marketing Association, 1120 Ave. of the Americas, New York, NY 10036, (212) 768-7277, fax: (212) 302-6714, www.the-dma.org

Independent Accountants International, email: info@accountants.org, www.accountants.org

International Association of Administrative Professionals (IAAP), 10502 NW Ambassador Drive, P.O. Box 20404, Kansas City, MO 64195, (816) 891-6600, fax: (816) 891-9118, email: service@iaap-hq.org, www.iaap-hq.org

International Association of Virtual Office Assistants (IAVOA), Route 1 Box 275, Red Oak, OK 74563, (918) 753-2716, fax: (918) 752-2717, e-mail: IAVOA@aol.com, www.iavoa.com

International Virtual Assistants Association (IVAA), 561 Keystone Ave, Suite 309, Reno, NV 89503, phone/fax: (888) 259-2487, www.ivaa.org

National Association for the Self-Employed, P.O. Box 612067, DFW Airport, Dallas, TX 75261, (800) 232-6273, fax: (800) 551-4446, www.nase.org

National Association of Home Based Businesses, 10452 Mill Run Cir., Owings Mills, MD 21117, (410) 363-3698, www.usahomebusiness.com

National Association of Professional Employee Organizations, 901 N. Pitt Street, #150, Alexandria, VA 22314, (703) 836-0466, fax: (703) 836-0976, e-mail: info@napeo.org, www.napeo.org

National Notary Association, 9350 De Soto Ave., P.O. Box 2402, Chatsworth, CA 91313, (800) US Notary (1-800-876-6827), fax: (800) 833-1211, e-mail: services@national notary.org, www.nationalnotary.org

National Resume Writers Association, P.O. Box 475, Tuckahoe, NY 10707, (877) THE-NRWA (1-877-843-6792), www.nrwa.com

Office Business Center Association International (formerly Executive Suite Association), 15000 Commerce Parkway, Suite C, Mount Laurel, NJ 08054, (800) 237-4741, fax: (856) 439-0525, e-mail: info@officebusinesscenters.com, www.officebusinesscenters.com

Professional Association of Resume Writers, 1388 Brightwaters Blvd., N.E., St. Petersburg, FL 33704, (800) 822-7279, fax: (727) 894-1277, e-mail: PARwhq@aol.com, www.parw.com

Service Corps of Retired Executives (SCORE) National Office, 409 Third St. SW, 6th Floor, Washington, DC 20024, (800) 634-0245, www.score.org

Small Business Administration, 409 Third St. SW, Washington, DC 20416, (800) 827-5722, www.sba.gov

Small Business Service Bureau, 544 Main Street, Worcester, MA 01615, (800) 343-0939, email: membership@sbsb.com, www.sbsb.com

Book Resources

Advertising on the Internet, Robbin Zeff and Bradley Aronson, John Wiley & Sons, www.wiley.com

The Chicago Manual of Style: The Essential Guide for Writers, Editors, and Publishers, University of Chicago Press

Editorial Freelancing: A Practical Guide, Trumbull Rogers, Aletheia Publications

Franchising and Licensing: Two Ways to Build Your Business, Andrew J. Sherman, Amacom

Get Smart! 365 Tips to Boost Your Entrepreneurial IQ, Rieva Lesonsky, Entrepreneur Magazine

Guerrilla Marketing for the Home-Based Business, Jay Conrad Levinson and Seth Godin, Houghton Mifflin

Home Businesses You Can Buy: The Definitive Guide to Exploring Franchises, Mult-Level Marketing and Business Opportunities, Plus How to Avoid Scams, Paul & Sarah Edwards and Walter Zooi, Putnam

How to Start a Home-Based Desktop Publishing Business, Louise Kursmark, Globe Pequot Press

How to Start a Home-Based Resume Business, Jan Melnik, CPRW, Globe Pequot Press

Making Money With Your Computer At Home: The Inside Information You Need to Know to Select and Operate a Full-Time, Part-Time or Add-On Business That's Right For You, Paul and Sarah Edwards, Tarcher Publishing

The McGraw-Hill 36-Hour Accounting Course, Robert. L. Dixon and Harold E. Arnett, McGraw-Hill Trade

Pricing Guide for Desktop Services, Fourth Edition, Robert Brenner, Brenner Information Group

Pricing Guide for Web Services, Robert Brenner, Brenner Information Group

Public Relations Kit for Dummies, Eric Yaverbaum and Bill Bly, Hungry Minds Inc.

Start and Run a Profitable Home-Based Business, Edna Sheedy, Self-Counsel Press

Start Your Own Business: The Only Start-Up Book You'll Ever Need, 4th Edition, Rieva Lesonsky, Entrepreneur Press

Start Your Own Consulting Service, John Riddle, Entrepreneur Press

Start Your Own E-Business, Robert McGarvy & Melissa Campanelli, Entrepreneur Press

Start Your Own Event Planning Business, Krista Turner, Entrepreneur Press

Start Your Own Medical Claims Billing Service, Rob and Terry Adams, Entrepreneur Press

Start Your Own Specialty Travel & Tour Business, Rob and Terry Adams, Entrepreneur Press

Ultimate Start-Up Directory, James Stephenson, Entrepreneur Press

The Vest Pocket CPA, Nicky A. Dauber, Joel G. Siegel and Jae K. Shim, Prentice Hall Press

The Virtual Office Survival Handbook: What Telecommuters and Entrepreneurs Need to Succeed in Today's Nontraditional Workplace, Alice Bredin, John Wiley & Sons

The World's Easiest Guide to Using the MLA: A User-Friendly Manual for Formatting Research Papers According to the Modern Language Association Style, Carol J. Amato, Stargazer Publishing Co.

Consultants and Other Experts

Robert S. Bernstein, Esq., Bernstein Bernstein Krawec & Wymard, P.C., 1133 Penn Ave., Pittsburgh, PA 15222, (412) 456-8100, fax: (412) 456-8135, e-mail: bob@bernsteinlaw.com

Biddle & Associates Inc., OPAC testing software (software to test typing speed/ accuracy, word-processing skills, language arts, math, financial skills, spreadsheets, databases and more), 2100 Northrop Ave., #200, Sacramento, CA 95825-3937, (800) 999-0438, fax: (916) 929-3307, www.opac. com, e-mail: staff@opac.com

Credit Services

American Express Merchant Services, (888) 829-7302, www.americanexpress.com

Discover Card Merchant Services, (800) 347-6673, http://discovernetwork.com/indexDM

First Data Merchant Services Corp. (provides credit-processing services), (800) 735-3362, www.firstdata.com

MasterCard, (914) 249-4843, www. mastercard.com

Tele-Check (provides check-guarantee services), (800) TELE-CHECK, www.telecheck.com

TransUnion (provides credit-reporting services), (800) 916-8800, www.transunion.com

Visa, (800) VISA-311, ext. 96, www. visa.com

Magazines and Publications

Accounting Office Management & Administration Report, 29 W. 35th Street, 5th Floor, New York, NY 10001, (212) 244-0360, www.ioma.com

Advertising/Communications Times, 123 Chestnut St., #202, Philadelphia, PA 19106, (215) 629-1666, fax: (215) 923-8358, www.adcommtimes.com

The Business Owner, 16 Fox Lane, Locust Valley, NY 11560, (516) 671-8100, fax: (516) 671-8099

Direct Marketing News, 100 Avenue of the Americas, New York, NY 10013, (212) 925-7300, fax: (212) 925-8752, www.dmnews.com

Entrepreneur Magazine, Entrepreneur Media Inc., 2445 McCabe Way, #400, Irvine, CA 92614, (949) 261-2325, www.entrepreneur.com

OfficePro magazine, International Association of Administrative Professionals, 5501 Backlick Rd., #240, Springfield, VA 22151-3940, (703) 914-9200, fax: (703) 914-6777, e-mail: officepromag@strattonpub.com

The Tax Advisor, Harborside Financial Center, 201 Plaza 3, Jersey City, NJ 07311-3881, (888) 777-7077, fax: (201) 521-5447, www.aicpa.org/pubs/taxadv/index.htm

Interviewed Successful Business Support Service Owners

Charlene Davis
4008 Waterview Loop
Winter Park, FL 32792
Phone: (407) 679-8119
Web site: www.cdavisfreelance.com
E-mail: cdmailbox@cdavisfreelance.com

Diana Ennen
Virtual Word Publishing
Phone: (954) 971-4025
Web site: www.virtualwordpublishing.com
E-mail: Diana@virtualwordpublishing.com

Gay Lynn Kirsch
Executive Secretarial Services, LLC
Phone: (703) 318-9511
Web site: www.execsecretarialsvs.com
E-mail: Execsecsvs@aol.com

Janice Byer
Docu-Type Administrative & Web Design Services
Phone: (519) 941-9523
Web site: www.docutype.net
E-mail: jbyer@docutype.net

Jill Chongva
Virtual Assistant Diva Administrative Services
Phone: (204) 470-8284
Web site: www.vadiva.com
E-mail: diva@vadiva.com

Kathie Thomas
"A Clayton's Secretary"®
Web site: www.vadirectory.net
E-mail: Kathie@vadirectory.net

Kimberley Thomas Catanzaro
Bookkeeping & Secretarial Services
Phone: (561) 741-2139
Web site: www.on-linesecretary.com
E-mail: Kim@on-linesecretary.com

Lyn Prowse-Bishop, MVA, ASO
Executive Stress Office Support
Web site: www.execstress.com
E-mail: Lyn@execstress.com
Skype: execstress

Lynne Norris
Norris Business Solutions
Phone: (814) 236-0523
Web site: www.norrisbusinesssolutions.com
E-mail: NorBusSol@pennswoods.net

Michelle Schoen
The Permanent Record
Phone: (303) 733-0885
Web site: www.thepermanentrecord.net
E-mail: Michelle.Schoen@thepermanentrecord.net

Michelle Ulrich
The Virtual Nation
Phone: (916) 536-9799
Web site: www.thevirtualnation.com

Sharon Williams
The 24 Hour Secretary
Alliance for Virtual Businesses
Web site: www.the24hoursecretary.com or www.allianceforvirtualbiz.com
E-mail: Sharon@the24hoursecretary.com or Info@allianceforvirtualbiz.com

Sherry Watkins
Go2REassistant
Phone: (334) 320-7486
Web site: www.Go2REassistant.com
E-mail: Sherry@Go2REassistant.com

Joann Voss
Voss Transcriptions Inc.
39 S. LaSalle Street, Suite 800
Chicago, IL 60603
Phone: (312) 346-3227
Fax: (312) 346-1199
Web site: www.vosstranscription.com
E-mail: vosstrans@aol.com

Bill Pypes
WordCare
575 Juniper Street
North Liberty, IA 52317
Phone: (319) 665-8333
E-mail: WordCare@aol.com

Surveyed Successful
Business Support Service Owners

Alana Daniels
Creative Resources—The Virtual Admin Office
Phone: (910) 353-0986
Web site: www.theadminoffice.com
E-mail: Alana@theadminoffice.com

Carlos Jones
Interoffice Solutions
Web site: www.interoffice-solutions.com
E-mail: Cjones@interoffice-solutions.com

Carol Deckert
Carol Deckert, Virtual Assistant
Phone: (717) 394-6452
E-mail: Caroldeckert@comcast.net

Caroline Jarzabek
CMJ Virtual Office Manager
Web site: www.clickawayva.com
E-mail: Caroline@clickawayva.com

Cheryl K. Callighan, MVA
eOffice-Virtual Assistants LLC

University of Virtual Assistants
Phone: (303) 347-2923
Web site: www.eoffice-virtualassist.com or www.uofvas.com
E-mail: Cheryl@eoffice-virtualassist.com or Cheryl@uofvas.com

Danielle Keister
The Relief Virtual Assistance
Phone: (253) 238-1368
Web site: www.therelief.com
E-mail: Service@therelief.com

Darcy Meinke
DLM Virtual Solutions
Phone: (402) 826-4118
Web site: www.dlmvirtualsolutions.com
E-mail: Darcy@dlmvirtualsolutions.com

Debbie Corlet
Deb-e-Secretarial
Web site: www.deb-e-secretarial.com.au
E-mail: Deb@deb-e-secretarial.com.au

Diana Ennen
Virtual Word Publishing
Phone: (954) 971-4025
Web site: www.virtualwordpublishing.com
E-mail: Diana@virtualwordpublishing.com

Doreen Patrick
Virtual Business Partners
Phone: (630) 541-2433
Web site: www.virtualbusinesspartners.net
E-mail: Ihireybp@sbcglobal.net

Gay Lynn Kirsch
Executive Secretarial Services, LLC
Phone: (703) 318-9511
Web site: www.execsecretarialsvs.com
E-mail: Execsecsvs@aol.com

Jan Clark
EVA-Electronic Virtual Assistant
Phone: (970) 252-8348
Web site: www.eva-colo.com
E-mail: Jan@eva-colo.com

▲

Janice Byer
Docu-Type Administrative & Web Design Services
Phone: (519) 941-9523
Web site: www.docutype.net
E-mail: jbyer@docutype.net

Jennifer Gniadecki
The Atypical VA
Phone: (708) 957-1479
Web site: www.atypicalva.com
E-mail: Jennifer@atypicalva.com

Jill Chongva
Virtual Assistant Diva Administrative Services
Phone: (204) 470-8284
Web site: www.vadiva.com
E-mail: diva@vadiva.com

Kathie Thomas
"A Clayton's Secretary"®
Web site: www.vadirectory.net
E-mail: Kathie@vadirectory.net

Kimberley Thomas Catanzaro
Bookkeeping & Secretarial Services
Phone: (561) 741-2139
Web site: www.on-linesecretary.com
E-mail: Kim@on-linesecretary.com

Lanel Taylor
Taylored Office Solutions
Phone: (208) 816-4257
Web site: www.tayloredofficesolutions.com
E-mail: Lanel@tayloredofficesolutions.com

Leza Cummins
Written Communications Specialties
Phone: (208) 457-1846
E-mail: Lezacummins@verizon.net

Lisa Humphries
Freelance PA
Web site: www.freelancepa.com.au
E-mail: Lisa@freelancepa.com.au

Lisa Wells
Coast2Coast Business Support Solutions
Web site: www.coast2coastbusiness.com
E-mail: Lisawells@coast2coastbusiness.com

Lori Davis
Davis Virtual Assistants
Phone: (518) 725-1688
Web site: www.davisva.com
E-mail: Lori@davisva.com

Louise Pack
Assist You
E-mail: Assistyou@optusnet.com.au

Lynne Norris
Norris Business Solutions
Phone: (814) 236-0523
Web site: www.norrisbusinesssolutions.com
E-mail: NorBusSol@pennswoods.net

Lyn Prowse-Bishop, MVA, ASO
Executive Stress Office Support
Web site: www.execstress.com
E-mail: Lyn@execstress.com
Skype: execstress

Margaret Doescher
Virtual Assistance At Your Service
Phone: (713) 529-5750
E-mail: Med1va@sbcglobal.net

Mary Adelman
Green Star Services, LLC
Phone: (973) 713-8786
Web site: www.growwithgreenstar.com
E-mail: Madelman@growwithgreenstar.com

Michelle Church
Virtually Distinguished
Phone: (562) 889-5742
Web site: www.virtuallydistinguished.com
E-mail: Virtuallydistinguished@charter.net

▲

Michelle Murphy
Murphy Assistants
Phone: (215) 310-9793
Web site: www.murphyassistants.com
E-mail: Michelle@murphyassistants.com

Michelle Schoen
The Permanent Record
Phone: (303) 733-0885
Web site: www.thepermanentrecord.net
E-mail: Michelle.Schoen@thepermanentrecord.net

Michelle Ulrich
The Virtual Nation
Phone: (916) 536-9799
Web site: www.thevirtualnation.com

Nikki White
Scribes Secretarial Services
Web site: www.scribes.net.au
E-mail: Nikki@scribes.net.au

Pamela A. Hunter
Creative Office Services
Phone: (410) 635-8500
Web site: www.creativeofficeservice.com
E-mail: Phunter1@creativeofficeservice.com

Sharon Williams
The 24 Hour Secretary
Alliance for Virtual Businesses
Web site: www.the24hoursecretary.com or www.allianceforvirtualbiz.com
E-mail: Sharon@the24hoursecretary.com or Info@allianceforvirtualbiz.com

Sherry Watkins
Go2REassistant
Phone: (334) 320-7486
Web site: www.Go2REassistant.com
E-mail: Sherry@Go2REassistant.com

Simone Christoph
SimOne Virtual Solutions
Phone: (505) 437-5070
Web site: www.simonevirtualsolutions.com
E-mail: Simone@simonevs.com

Tara Truax
Type It
Phone: (509) 899-1566
Web site: www.typeitoffice.com
E-mail: Typeitteam@yahoo.com

Terri Orlowski
Beyond the Office
Web site: www.beyondtheoffice.com
E-mail: Terri@beyondtheoffice.com

Vickie Turley
Elite Virtual Assistants
Phone: (270) 495-4737
Web site: www.elitevas.com
E-mail: Vturley@elitevas.com

Wendy Weightman
Weightman Typing & Design
Web site: www.wtyping.com.au
E-mail: Wendy@wtyping.com.au

Web Resources

1ShoppingCart.com: Shopping Cart Software, Ecommerce Solutions and Internet

AJIAtrain.com: AJIA offers a Virtual Assistant Software Training Track Program

AllianceForVirtualBiz.com: Alliance for Virtual Businesses™

ATAContact.org: American Telemarketing Association

Business.gov: Official Business Link to the U.S. Government

CanadianVA.net: Canadian Virtual Assistant Network

Docutype.net/BecomeaVA.htm: Becoming a VA by Docu-Type

FactFinder.census.gov: American FactFinder

GoToMyPC.com: Remote PC Access Anywhere

IAVOA.com: International Association of Virtual Office Assistants

IAAP-HQ.org: International Association of Administrative Professionals

IVAA.org: International Virtual Assistants Association

LogMeIn.com: Remote PC access and backup

▲

Marketingpower.com: American Marketing Association

NFIB.com: Small Business Economic Trends & Polls

NFWBO.org: Center for Women's Business Research

NWBC.gov: National Women's Business Council

OfficeBusinessCenters.com: Office Business Center Association International

OIVAC.com: Online International Virtual Assistant Convention

REVAnetwork.com: The Premier Real Estate Virtual Assistant Network

SBA.gov: U.S. Small Business Administration

SCORE.org: Service Corps Of Retired Executives: Counselors to America's Small Business

TraxTime.com: Personal punch clock software to track billable hours.

VACertification.com: Virtual Assistant Certification (MVA)

VAconference.com: Industry conference from the leaders in virtual assistance.

VANetworking.com: Virtual Assistant Networking Association (VANA) & Forum

VANetworking.com/virtual-assistant-business: Virtual Business Start Up System

VASummit.org: IVAA Professional Virtual Assistant's Best Practice Conference

VA-theseries.com: Virtual Assistant—The Series

VATrainer.com: VA Coaching & Education from "A Clayton's Secretary"®

VirtualAssistanceU.com: Virtual Assistance U for global VA training

VirtualAssistantStartups.com: How to Be a VA by Virtual Word Publishing

VSSCyberOffice.com/VBO: Virtual Business Owners' Training Program VBO

Work-The-Web.com: Virtual Assistance E-Zine

Appendix B

IVAA/IAVOA Registered Business Support Service Directory by State

Here are some registered business support service owners listed by state who have posted their contact information only for referrals and networking, not for sales calls. For current contact information for these businesses, check out their listings on the International Virtual Assistants Association's site, www.ivaa.org or the International Association of Virtual Office Assistants' site, www.iavoa.com.

Alabama

Brown Virtual Assistance: Lane H. Brown
Go2REassistant: Sherry Watkins
My Cyber Assistant: Michelle Mathews
Tiger Virtual Assistance: Tillie G. Sita

Alaska

K. Burgess Consulting: Kathy Burgess

Arizona

AAA: VerySmartPeople Inc.: Pamela Andersen
Coordinator Group: Karen Drebes
Creative Agent Solutions: Sarah R. Reiter
CynAssist, LLC: Cindy Nilles

East Phoenix Secretarial: Maureen Townsend
GAP Virtual Assistant, Inc.: Jeanna G. Garrett
Gotcha Secretarial Services: Betsy Mason
Loose Ends: Katie Baird
Office Support Services: Judy Vorfeld
Queen Assistant Virtual Administrative Services: Denise N. Campbell
Richins Business Support Solutions: Laura Jo Richins
Second Self Office Assistance: Pamela Cendejas
Servitium, LLC: Sharon J. Simpson
Virtually Yours Secretarial Services: Karan Faris
Winning Edge Business Services: Rebecca Gladden

Arkansas

SOHO Business Solutions: Donna Gunter
Your Virtual Secretary: Julie Wilson

California

4officeassistance.com: Janet McIntosh
Acumen VA: Mia C. Chambers
Admin At Your Service: Paula A. Farthing
AdminPro: Robin Sagara
American River College: Roietta Fulgham
ArlynBaggot.biz: Arlyn Baggot
ARTech Virtual Services: Janylyn Marks
Ask-My VA: Arlene Wolfe
Ascend Business Solutions: Scott Barrella
Assist-Net: Lisa Leete
A Virtual Affair: Shelley M. Owens
Bannister Business Services: Karen Bannister
Barbara's Word—Your Virtual Partner: Barbara Dennis
Baty's Business e-Support Services: Patricia Baty
Benjamin Un-Limited: S. Darlene Benjamin
Blossom Hill Secretarial Services: Jane Danen
Craig Hart Consulting, LLC: Sydni C. Craig-Hart
Creative Admin Services: Melissa Kuhuski
Creative Partner Business Coaching: Petra Jakobskrueger
CyberQueen Virtual Office: Ana Lucia Medeiros
Cybertary: Patricia M. Beckman
Datatrek Computer Services: Sharon Deutsch
Deadline Data: Jeannie Hathaway
Delegate It VA: Delores Abrams

Details Virtual Assisting: Kristine R. Cataldo
Direct Mail Services: Karen Hebert
DoubleU Virtually: Wolfram Weinberg
Dreams & Vision: Tasha Chimienti
Dynamic Support Solutions: Sandra Silva
Elk Grove Virtual Assistant: Meredith Piggee
Emerald City Virtual Solutions: Laurie Mutch
Executive Administrative Support Services (EASS): Gloria J. Nelson.
Executive Virtual Assistant Services: Roberta E. Eastman, GVA
First Class Virtual Assisting: Julie Coffman
Foor Creative: N. Joanna Foor
Green Office Solutions: Sharon Broughton
Greystone Virtual Business Services: Judith Groover Stein
Information Tracking Systems, Inc.: Debra Kalmon
Jammin Business Solutions: Julee Ellison
JMS Business Assistance: Janis M. Salvi
Kaydee Bookkeeping Services: Kathryn Louise Donath
KDO Virtual Assistance: Kirsten D. O'Keefe
Key Office Specialists: Kathleen Omi
KM Consulting: Kelly Minton
La Costa Virtual Assistants: Jacqueline McGinnis
Lighthouse Travel & Tours: Donna C. West
MBA: My Brilliant Assistant!: Cheralind Smith Green
Meg Dastrup's Word Power Plus: Meg Dastrup
Miracle Assistant: Stacey T. Normandy
Nazila Moammtazei: Nazila L. Moammtazei
Nicorpa Client Services: Nichola Mente
Nina Feldman Connections: Nina Feldman
O'Dell Business Services: Lisa O'Dell-Nin
Orange County Virtual Assistance: Susan Markow
Pacific Pro Virtual Assistant: Gretchen H. Walden
Professional Assistant Services: Charmaine Gapuz
Ramey Virtual Assistance: Margie Ramey
ReGraphix: Herbert Rubinstein
RJ's Word Processing Services: Rita Cartwright
Ruth Roybal, Virtual Assistant: Ruth Roybal
Santa Barbara Virtual Assistants: Cheryl L. Ebner
Shammah C.A.S.T. Corp: Andrea Berry
SimpAssist Business Solutions: Lisa Ramsey-Simpson
Simply Sharon Virtual Assistant: Sharon Broughton
Sooter Consulting & Admin. Services: Donna M. Sooter

▲

Susan Showers Secretarial Services: Susan R. Showers
Tina's Business Solutions: Tina M. Carter
Transaction Coordination Services: Stephanie C. McKenzie
U Need Us 123: Fau Hudson
Virtual Exec Solutions: Nancy Seley
Virtual Legal Assist: Caara T. Sinclaire
Virtually Built: Sharon Harrison
Virtually Distinguished: Michelle C. Church
Virtually Taken Care Of! Inc.: Wendy F. Terrado
Virtual Nation: Michelle Ulrich
Virtual PA Solutions: Kim Guglielmino
Virtual Sales Assistance: Catherine Schooling
Virtual Simplicity: Sally Kuhlman
YGF Services: Misty Taylor
Your VAssistant: Charlestine Pride
Your Virtual EA: Dominique E. Blake

Colorado

AAA Office Support: Ann Schurig
Allison Business Solutions: Carol Allison
Andrea Kalli Virtual Trainer and Assistant, LLC: Andrea Kalli
Berg Business Solutions, Inc.: Gretchen Berg
Carrollegal: Lynn R. Carroll
Colorado Virtual Assistant Group: Jessica L. Chaffin
Coppertree Desktop Services: Tracy M. McIlrath
C.Y. Virtual Solutions: Charlotte L. Lingard-Young
Envision Business Services: Rosemarie Camacho
EOffices-Virtual Assistants: Cheryl Calligan
EVA: Electronic Virtual Assistant: Jan Clark
Executive Assistance Live!: Pamela G. Nash
Executive Services, LLC: Laurel Foster
Girl Friday Rescue: Amy Mathews
I Can Do That!: Lois H. Feinstein
Integrity Creative Business Solutions: Connie J. Schlosberg
JenAssist: Jennifer Iler
JERPAT: Patty Benton
Pikes Peak Virtual Assistant Group: Jana L. Wegelin
Ritchie Secretarial Service: Kathy Ritchie
Satellite Business Solutions: Susan H. Shilling
Taylor by Design: Ronda J. Taylor
V-and-E- Services: Karen Reddick

VIP Secretarial Services: Susan Ackerman
Virtual Officeworks: Julie Johnson
White River Virtual Solutions: Melody Scritchfield
Your Virtual Assistant, LLC: Linda K. Sinclair
Your Virtual Jeannie: Jeannie Byford

Connecticut

HELP Virtual Office Support: Mary LaFrance
LEIDERS Consulting: Kristine K. Leitch
Schiff and Schiff Communications: Jennifer L. Schiff
SOS Technology Group, LLC: Linda Phillips
Today's Administrative Solutions: Jennifer D. Rai
Virtually Done by Vickie: Vickie Hadge

Delaware

DesqTop Office Solutions: Valerie D. Hall
Just Your Type Service: Linda DiCamillo
Virtual Assistant Done Right: Monroe M. Alicia

Florida

Access Property Network, LLC: Mary Zabala
All Notary Services: Christina Brewer
Alternative Office Support: Debbie Peshek
Assurance Business Solutions: Cristina Jimenez
Bonman Solutions: Bonnie Grossman
Bookkeeping & Secretarial Services: Kimberley Thomas Catanzaro
Bostler, Inc.: Arva Butler
Clarity Transactions: Victoria A. Santiago
Delegate It Virtual Assistant Services: Kara Wierzbowski
Divine Learning Solutions, Inc.: Nicole Townsend
E admin: Dawn Stebbins
Elena Darcy: Virtual Assistant: Eleana D'Arcy
ELS Virtual Solutions: Evy Schwartz
Ennen's Computer Service: Diana Ennen
Errands Around Town: Judy L Rutkowski
Exclusive Concepts Concierge, Inc.: Denetrya S. Brookins
ExecuStuff Services: Heather C. Dady
Executive Assisting: Dorian Pagnanella
Exquisite Secretarial Services: Stacy Shaw-Virgo
Gulf Coast Office Support: Jama St. John
Hascall's Virtual World: Susan Hascall

Husebo Virtual Assistance: Lisa Husebo
JoLain Virtual Assistant Services: Joanne Lain
McGuirePro Marketing Agency: Jean M. McGuire
MoriahLR: Darcey F. Grainer & Moriah L. Rocha
Mouse Works, Inc: Cheryl Tittle
MPE Assistance: Nancy S. Messer
My Perfect Assistant, Inc.: Pollyanna Mailhot
My Real Estate VA: Angela K. Simanek
Northside Office Solutions: Jan E. Ream
O'Brien Business Services: Denise M. O'Brien
OTR Group Corporation: Francisco E. Centeno
Private Virtual Assistant, A: Sandy Lovig
ProExecs, Inc.: Anisa A. Turner
Progressive Publishing Services: Janice Wlodarski
SFL Virtual Office Assistants, Inc: Sarah Saladino
Simple Solutions in Real Estate: Ulee Forrest
Software Made Easy, LLC: Kimberly C. Lanners
Streamline Office Solutions: Christine C. Fuller
Top Priority: Shelly's Virtual Office Support, The: Shelly A. Woodum
Virtual Essentials: Eleisa Walker
Virtual INNsider.com: Monika Trenkler
Virtually Ready: Lisa S. Schultz
Virtually Solved: Kathryn Hadzibajric
Virtual Solution, A: Shannon R. Adams
Virtual Office. The: Jonni Anderson
Virtual Online Solutions, Inc.: Cari Gonzalez
Virtual Word Publishing: Diana L. Ennen
Williams Virtual Solutions: Regina L. Williams

Georgia

AKM Administrative Services: Alicia Marston
All Empowered, Inc.: Melanie Magruder
Andrea Pixley, Virtual & Personal Assistant: Andrea Pixley
AnotherME: Patty G. Keller
A Plus Virtual Assistance: Donna Elliott
Boundless Virtual Solutions: Melissa Dillard
Brochures By Design.com: Evalyn M. Williams
Casey & Company: Honey R. Casey
CIJ Administrative Services: Gabriela Sanchez
Destiny Group Professional Office Management, A: Alison Jackson
Diversified Business Solutions: Tina Price

DocuDoc Virtual Assistant: Sue Wood
Executive Assistants Solutions, LLC: Marlena Thomas
Expert Business Solutions, Inc.: Karyn Huggins
Full Spectrum Consulting: Bonnie L. Claggett
Global Events Emporium: Shandrolyn Bell
Helen Smith: Virtual Assistant: Helen Smith
IDP Services: Vicki Steppe
Janice Kyle-Walker: Master Virtual Assistant: Janice Kyle-Walker
Monarch Business Solutions, Inc.: Lisa Spruck
Noble Solutions: Eleanor Doty
Personal Assistant Services: Lori J. Barlow
Professional Legal Services: M. Gail Bailey
Realty Support Plus: Melinda L. Runkle
Serenity Business Solutions, LLC: Antonette Benford
Six Cents Enterprises: Tangerine Goodwin
Smary Imaging: Latachia Williams-Coleman
SpyderArt Web Services: Beth Bovard
T.A.P. Business Services: Angela Curvin
TheMortgageVA.com: Jackie Kiadii
Type*4*U: Jackie Love
VECoordinator: Star V. Smith
Virtual Desk, A: Donielle Mitchner
Virtual SOHO Solution: Jivonne Gilliam
Your Own Virtual Assistant: Debbie Fung-A-Wing

Hawaii

Admin To Go: Phyllis Seymour

Idaho

All Digital Designs: Kendall D Gjevre
Essential Admin: Amber Drake
Taylored Office Solutions: Lanel C. Taylor
Top Seller Sites: Kevin Harper
Virtual Assistant Associates: Tabitha Funk
Virtually Everything: Barbara Rowen
Your Administrative Solutions: Fran S. McCully

Illinois

1st Class Virtual Administrative Assistance: Marie McCurley
Aardvark Web Works: Marlene Frykman
Accredited Virtual Assistance: Jacqueline DeBoer

▲

AdminiSource Now: Deanne Splear
Allsot Advantage, The: Kathy Allsot
Another 8 Hours: Kelly Poelker
Assistants At Their Best: Jacqueline M. Clark
Atisor Business Solutions: Anne Marie R. Davidson
Chameleon Office Pros: Heidi Saeter
Charlotte Street: Pat Walsh
Clarity Virtual Assistance: Robin Courchesne-Sato
Dedicated Secretarial Services, Inc.: Linda Catomer
Everything Virtual: Heather Hein
Infinite Business Solutions: Patti M. Ciccone & Karen A. Randel
LG Concepts: Linda G. Bomya
Lindaahudson.com: Linda A. Hudson
Michigan Avenue Office Services, Inc.: Marilyn Hallett Granzyk
MoPoe & Associates: Monica L. Poe
NASCO, LLC: Roshanda L. Neal
NuVo Partners: Melissa A. Vokoun
Office Grapevine, The: Catherine Mallers
Organizing Solutions, Inc.: Pamela Colovos
Osage Enterprises: Tom Lamm
Out of Office, Inc.: Kimberly Kissel
Peace of Mind Virtual Assistance: Sue Kramer
Premiere Business Solutions: Rebecca M. Albertini
Premiere Small Business Assistance: Robin L. Kramer
RealSupport, Inc.: Carrie Gable
Shadow Executive Services: Sandra M. Roos
Techie Temps: Melissa Guajardo
Timeless Professional Assisting & Consulting Service: Christina Haberstich
Time Squared: "Less to do. More time for you.": Lisa Arvanites
Virtual Business Partners: Doreen R. Patrick
Virtual Business & Real Estate Services: Vivian Little
Virtually Fantastic: Cindy Gaffen
World Class Concierge Service, Inc.: Teresa A. Frith
Your Assistant Business Solutions: Ron Stempkowski

Indiana

All-Write Virtual Office: Clara Fyffe
A.M. Assist, LLC: Amy Morris
Decker Office Services, VA: June R. Decker
Four Seasons Virtual Assistance: Debra M. Higgins
On Demand Business Solutions: Your Real Estate Virtual Assistant: Mary Salewske

Professional's Right Hand, The: Christy Villas
Under1Roof Administrative Services, LLC: Patti M. Marshall, MBA
Virtual Office Solution: Cynthia T. Sacchini

Iowa

Karen Seltrecht Virtual Assistant: Karen Seltrecht
Karyn's Toolkit: Karyn Stille
Konceptuality: Karen S. McGreevey
LampStone Office Solutions: Pamela S. Crome
Reinhardt Virtual Assistants: Chantal Reinhardt
Wedmore Virtual Assistants: Sandra Wedmore

Kansas

ALC Office Services, LLC: Anne L. Camien
Your Professional Business Solution: Pam Hair

Kentucky

Accu-Assist: Angela R. Smith
Anything Virtually: Martina D. Lucas
Deb's Desk: Debbie Burns
Mark It Done Virtual Assistant Service: Rosemary Yourtee

Louisiana

Administrative Services of New Orleans: Marilyn Kline
Realty Link, The: Keesha Broussard

Maryland

The 24 Hour Secretary: Sharon Williams
AMH Business Solutions: Ann M. Harrell
Angie Assist Virtual Purchasing & Business Support: Angie Hodges
Barefoot Office Solutions, LLC: Theresa M. Chiovaro
BranJor Solutions, Inc.: Alicia White-Kelly
Creative Computer Concepts, Inc.: Bonnie Costley
Creative Office Services: Pamela Hunter
Cyber Assistant, The: Carol B. Cormany
A Different View: Lynn M. Crawford
Exceptional Business Solutions: Tya Bolton
First Choice Administrative Solutions: Valerie Holland
Freeland Office Assistant Outsource Center: Hope M. Adeoye
Hallmark Virtual Solutions: Sharen Favre
Handy Business Solutions: Trenell A. McCauley

▲

iRealStar Business Services, LLC: Valentino M. Capone
iVirtual Assistant: Angie Hodges
Jaelyn's LLC: Sheila R. B. Singleton
JW Virtual Office Services: Judy Wilson
Lee Office and Computer Services: Monica Lee
Luce Creek Associates: Jo Anne W. Schram
M. Alexander & Associates, Inc.: Marleen Alexander
Mosaic Business Solutions, LLC: Amy Bradbury
My Business Assistant: Devina Mahapatra
RH Business Support: Rosemarie Harvey
Rsum Design & Graphics: Roddie Taylor
Simply Assisted: Jessica M. Britto
Smart Office Solutions, Inc: Bonita Telford
Sussman Company: Jill A. Sussman
Task Fairy: Marvel Jones
Office Masters: Danielle N. Moser
Vaughanwalt Consulting Services: Fiona Elizabeth Vaughans
Vine International: Natasha L. Suber
Virtual Administrative Services (VAS): Becky Gregory
Virtual Assistance4You: A Service of Xcalibur Solutions, Inc.: Peg Vanderlipp
Virtually Detailed: Rebecca L. Beauman
Virtually Yours Personal Assistants: Vernise Bolden
Your Home Office: Dawn Fowler

Massachusetts

Boston Virtual Solution, The: Sandra P. Martini
Broadway Business Services: Kathy Finklestein
Consider It Done Virtual Assistance Services: Sandra Giusti
Cybersecretary, The: Mary C. Pierce
Daybreak Enterprises: Dawn D. Hekking
Effective Office Services: Cheryl Alstrom
EmpireAdmin Corporation: Suzanne Boyd
Hansard Solutions: Jennifer Hansard
Left Margin Noted: Deborah Thomas
MLR Assist: Mary Weaver
Office Essentials by Sharon: Sharon Donahue
Town & Country Concierge, LLC: Virginia Snyder
Virtual Business Services: Tina DiMeo
Your IP Paralegal: Diane Miles

Michigan

3H Virtual Services: Michelle Hutter
A Little Executive Assistance: Lisa Hern
Assistance From A Distance: Tracey Dye
Assistant 2 U: Robin K Andrasi
Blue Water Assistant: Rita G. Roehrig
Dawn Laney, VA: Dawn M. Laney
Digital Designs by Eileen: Eileen Epstein
Elite Business Support, Inc.: Donna Gaither
Global Connection Virtual Office: Beverly King
Instant Assistant, Inc.: Monica Archibald
Kaisana Administrative Support: Sherly Michilli
K.S.J. Marketing Communications, LLC: Kimberley S. Johnson
Mank's Design Co.: Rachael Smith
MJE Associates: Joyce Edwards
Mid-Knight Business Solutions: Michelle M. Knight
Progressive Office Solutions: Paula Marie Woolley
Simply Virtual: Nikita Allen
Transcription Team, The: Dawn McLatcher
Virtual Partnering: Cindy Hillsey, CPVA
Your Ideal Office: Tena Kinsel
Your Professional Assistant: Randi Tucker Barr

Minnesota

Anthony Office Solutions: Holly M. Anthony
Attache, Inc.: Margaret P. Fowler
Dave's VA Service: David R. Anderson
Extended Office: Angie Schaefbauer
Humility Publishing: Sister Vida Barr
Laurie Klepinger Business Services: Laurie Klepinger
Optimus Virtual Assistants: Stephanie A. Haggerty
VA Office Solution: Jean Hanson
Web Executive Assistant: Pamela Akkerman

Mississippi

Annointed Assistant: Christine M. Davis
Signature Worx, LLC: Connie McVicker
Virtual Office Solutions & Services, LLC: Elaine T. Brown

▲

Missouri

Accurate Business Services: Jeannine Clontz
Admin Professionals on Demand: Lynn M. Taylor
Bar JD Communications: Judith A. Lorenz
Competitive Computer Resource: Amy G. Kesler
Creative Support Solutions: Sandra Lynn
eSolutions By Valerie: Valerie Gallup
Golden Services Group: Julie Eudy
LP Professionals: Linda Paul
Quality Business Solutions, LLC:Tricia Kos
Renaissance Small Business Services: Adrienne O. Backus
Secretary Center: Deana L. Cain
SlipStream Data Solutions: Milady Bryan
Wordstation: Margaret Robinson
Young VA Outsourcing Services: Bridget L. Young

Montana

E-Sistant: Sonya L. Mapp
KinSites, LLC: Liz Watson
Mountain Solutions: Peggy McCabe-Schmitz
Transaction Savvy: Holly Olson
Virtual Web Assistant: Varju Luceno

Nebraska

AdminPro Connections: Danielle Ruffin
DLM Virtual Solutions: Darcy L. Meinke
HINZ Business Services: Glenda Hinz

Nevada

Advantage One: The Write Business: Jacqueline M Simmons
ASBP: Penny Redgrave
Business Sense: A Virtual Association: Marie Molik
DidaVa.com, LLC: Jarita Clifton
Divine Solutions: Menyone Thomas
Executive Assistance International: Raquel Nilson
LMD Virtual Solutions: Lisa M. Dunaga
Office Elite: Vanessa Berry
Smart Solutions: Shari Shipman
Virtual Executive Assistant: Raquel Nilson
Your Admin Pro: Jan Cummings

New Hampshire

Affinity Virtual Assistance, LLC: Susan K. Peel
DLS Virtual Assistance: Donna L. Sopper
Goutiere Professional Business Services: Ramona Goutiere
Virtual Admin Online: Amanda L. Sage
Virtual Market Support: Lyn Raia Toomey

New Jersey

Abigail Nathan Business Services: Susan H. Markens
Above & Beyond, Inc.: Donna Miller
Accurate Assistance: Lisa M. Tuccillo
Administrative Solutions by Lysa: Lysa M. Delefeti
Aline Saba, CMP: Aline Saba
Allison Lane Business Solutions: Jackie Eastwick
Assist U, LLC: Cindy Colucci
Avertua, LLC: Alyssa M. Gregory
Barber Virtual Assisting Solutions, LLC: Megan Barber
Barrister Plus Typing, Ltd: Lynn R. Cipriani
Better Biz Services: Gail Somers
Burgo Virtual Office Assistance: Lorie Ann Burgo
Capital Solution, A: Joy Slaughter
Cairns Creative Services: Jane A. Cairns
ConsultingRUs: Jenny Jimenez
Cushing Designs: Fae Cushing
Delegate: Emily C. Morgan
Green Star Services: Mary P. Adelman
Laste Professional Resources: Stephanie Laste
Lynne J. Administrative Assistant: Lynne M. Jamiolkoski
Mantz Support Services: Betty Mantz
My eBusiness Solutions: Dorothy Meyer Monigan
PS: We Assist: Pamela Braue
Randolph Virtual Assistants: Nancy L. Randolph
Simply-Perfection: Rhonda Stuckey
Third Hand Secretarial Service: Linda Siniscal
VirtualEntertainmentSecretary.com: Michelle Thomas-Hanson
Virtual Legal Assistant, The: Aretha A. Gaskin
Virtual Officemate Consulting: Colleen Tracey
Words in Process: Nancy Eliot
Wright Solution, The: Caroline Wright

New Mexico

Able Admin and Voice Services: Rosemary Metcalf
APA2 Creative Virtual Assistance, LLC: Kimberli A. Werner
Player Office Solutions: Joan Simpson
SimOne Virtual Solutions: Simone Christoph
Virtual E-ssistant Solutions: Heather Hill
Your VaPro.net: Janice St. Germain, MVA

New York

Admin Help: Ana M. Hernandez
Confrar, Virtual Assistant Service: Connie Frary
Dahlia Web Designs LLC: Dahlia Benaroya
Davis Virtual Assistants: Lori Davis
DC Solutions 4U: Deidre Davis
Define Type Word Processing Services: Sharon Burns
Expert Admin: Elayne Morga
Exponential Business Solutions: Heather R. Chapman
Freedom Virtual Assistance: Ann Dick
Global VpA, LLC: Yasmina F. Edwards
Hindman QuickType Service: Patti D. Hindman
Innovative Executive Assistance: Michele Luxenberg
K A P Services: Kelly A. Pilonero
LBS Business Services: Linda B. Selden
LegalTypist, Inc.: Andrea Cannavina
N'suta Virtual Support Services: Odessia Nsafoah
NYvirtualassistant.com: La Tarisha Garbutt
Office Services of Orange County: Christine Pritchard
Officewaves: Paolina LoCicero
RealEstateShows.com: Michael C. Hogan
Real Time Assistance: Georgina B. Insdorf
RequestWorks: Melissa A. Keefe
Secret Assistant, The: Jeri C. Winkler
The Other Office: Zita Vlismas
Type-Right, Inc.: Van K. Morrow
Versatile Virtual Assistant: Andrea Mercado
Virtual Assistance...From a Distance: Ryland Jordan
Virtual Assistant Business Solutions: Carole L. Utter
Workstation: Laura Leites

North Carolina

Accelerate Your Business: Cathi Smith

Accurate Admin Services: Kathleen Lindsey
ANR Group, The: Janee Nelson
Coast2Coast Business Support Solutions: Lisa R. Wells
DeskTop VA: Carolyn S. Nelson
eOffice Solutions: Diane E. Barnes
Global Business Solutions: Rochelle J. Hull
iAssist Virtual Services: Melissa A. Boyd
InSources: Anik Aminuddin
International Executive Choice: Virtual Assistants and Consulting: Maria E. Stahli
MCC Services: Gail M. Hrdlicka
Outer Banks Real Estate Support: Shirley H. Williams
P&P Enterprises: Penny Timbie
Professional Assistance: Kristy Couch
Real Time Support: Patricia Jean Herron
S C Glenn & Associates: Stephanie Glenn
Virtually Accomplished: Latega Powell
Your Virtual Assistant: Belinda Smith
Zeteo Solutions: Lisa C. Boyd

North Dakota

Amy's Office: Amy Goble

Ohio

713Training.com: Victoria Ring
Ask This Man: Mitchell L. Muskin
At Your Service Cincinnati, Ltd.: Nora Rubinoff
Clerical Services Unlimited: Darlene S. Rager
Desai-Designs: Jayashree Paranjape
eOffice Support: Ann R. Nienaber
Fastype VA Services, Inc.: Terry L. Green
Jane's Virtual Office: Jane Rowe
Kathleen's Virtual Admin Services, LLC: Kathleen M. Finch
Kim Harte & Co. LLC: Kim Harte
MMR Business Solutions: Alicia R. Rittenhouse
My Efficient Assistant: Sandy L. Parker
Office Exchange, Inc.: Bunny Boerger
Parker Typing Service: Betty Parker
Real Estate Assistant, The: Tina Campbell
Task Away, Inc.: Camille Baron
TLC Secretarial Services: Claudia Salinger
Tracey Lawton Transcription & Admin: Tracey Lawton

Virtual Admins Plus: Ann Brown
Virtual Office Assist: Deanna Lange
Virtual Support: Betty L. Bowers
Virtuoso Administrative Services: Lisa Morgan

Oklahoma

GSR Virtual Solutions: Glenela S. Pajpaul
Poteau's Virtual Assistant: Alfred L. Gandee
Re/Max First: Elizabeth J. Burke

Oregon

Centerpointe Business Solutions: Juanita Amacher
Hettwer Virtual Office: Mary Hettwer
It's Virtually Done!: Kristy K. Schnabel
Miley Consulting, LLC: Deborah K. Miley
Victoria Prince eOffice Services: Victoria E. Prince
Virtual Assist On Call: Susan Lucibello

Pennsylvania

Ajia Training & Consulting Services, Inc.: Anita Pastor
Ballard Business Solutions: Sharon Ballard
Behind the Scenes VA: Kimberly D. Mann
Bricker Agency: Erika Bricker
Colorful Concepts: Kenneth Pezanowski
Core Office Solutions: Corie A. Stewart
Coyle on Call: Irene Souder-Coyle
Dynamic Virtual Assistant, Inc.: Anna Maria Granato
Elite Office Solutions, Inc.: Donna M. Littrell
Essential Support Services: Carolyn N. Kaminski
JB Document Services: Jan Beebe
Kondracki Business Services: Karen Kondracki
Henninge Medical Billing & Claims: Andrea Henninge
Hidden Helper, LLC: Lauren Hidden
Illuminated Designs: Char Diehm
Im-mack-ulate Impressions: Kirsten Womack
Innovate Services: Teresa Berger
Murphy Assistants: Michelle K. Murphy
Norris Business Solutions: Lynne Norris
Office DEVA: Laura Pumo
Office Magic USA: Carol J. Nicoletti
Pittsburgh P.A.s: Nancy Sukits

Pro-To-Type Services: Nancy E. Zatzman
ProVirtual Solutions: Mary Motz
Rogers Executive Administrative Services: Susan M. Rogers
Simms Consulting: Sheba T. Simms
Simplified Office Solutions: Errica C. Jamieson
Spiotto Virtual Assistant Services: Marlene Spiotto
That Girl Wednesday: Cynthia Utz
Virtual Business Solutions, LLC: Launa H. Post & Rebecca A. Ramsey
Virtual Business Support, LLC: Doreen Hartley
Virtually On It: Susan Kovalesky
VirtuallyTheOne: Kathy Zengolewicz
Virtual Office Solutions: Love Hubbard
Virtual Staff Solutions: Denise Watson
Wilson Virtual Assistants: Carla R. Wilson
Write On: Georgi Offrell

Rhode Island

Metko Administrative Services: Stefanie R. Metko
Your Island Concierge, LLC: Lynne Souza

South Carolina

Admin Link, The: Loretta Darby
An Assistant On Call: Nancy C. Ruben
Elsewhere, LLC: Lauri A. Bayless
Low Country Virtual Assistant: Marie Martinez
Professional Business Services: Craig D. Allen
Secretarial Solutions: Toni McNulty
VAAST (Virtual Administrative Assistant): Gwendolyn Y. Wright
Virtual Accuracy: Becki Noles
Virtual Business Solutions LLC: Jacqueline A. Powell

South Dakota

SOS ~ Simple Organized Solutions: Kristen Ham

Tennessee

A Great VA: Karen K. Valentine
Brooks Unlimited: Noble Brooks
Click Away VA, A: Kristy Worrell
Desktop Solutions: Jean Bunel
Elite Virtual Solutions: Janie Wilson
KSKruse Ultimate Office Solutions: Kim S. Kruse

Merrick Management and Media Services LLC: Taryn S. Merrick
Most Accurate Word Processing and VA Service: Rhonda Tate
Panacea Concepts: Julie B. Ensor
Professional Business Services: Linda Granito
Timesavers Virtual Office Assistance: Suzanne Burns
Valentine Virtual Services: Karen Valentine
Versassist: Virtual Support Solutions: Erin Scobee
VirtualMVPSTM.com: DJ Watson

Texas

1st Choice Virtual Solutions: Syvester Jordan
A2Z-Virtual Assistant, Inc.: Diann L. Black
ABV Enterprises: Vera Paine
Ace Transcription, Etc.: Sherrye L. Qualls
Admin Genie: Cristine Atkinson
Agent Services: Jeannette M. Marshall
All Thats Clerical: Anne Fifield
Alpha Omega Virtual Office: Joan Nash
A-Quality Virtual Support: Cyndi Wallace
Assistant For Hire: Laurie Bucci
Assistants For Agents, LLC: Cathryn Jones
Assuage Office Pros: Donnette Goheen Cowgill
AtkinsVA: Bonnie Atkins Saunders
Austin Virtual Management: Harmony Rogers
Business Mind VA: Cassandra D. Blakely
Cerebral Solutions: Helen G. Bell
Classic Real Estate VA: Gale Gallagher
Cmoore Virtual Office Solutions: Cathy Moore
Cole Connection Office Support Services: Rose G. Cole
Croft Virtual Solutions: Jaclyn M. Croft
Cybil-Khan Virtual Assistance: Sonia Akins
DFW Virtual Assistants, LLC dba VirtualAssistantsDFW.com: Gina Holloway
Earl of Scope Transcription: Wanda Hilliard
eAssistant Virtual Business Services: Mary E. Rowland
Engle Support Services: Heather A. Englebretson & Nancy A. Long
I'm Your Virtual Assistant: Johnnie Ruth Hamill
INVESP Virtual Assistants: Administrative and Writing Services: Ayat Shukairy
IQubed, Inc.: Cathy Z. Harrison
JWC Consulting: Jenny Claggett
Kim Hughes & Company: Kimberly Denise Hughes
Neibert's Virtual Assistance: Kristin A. Neibert

OffAssist: Candace E. Beauchamp
Pros & Commas: Donnette Goheen Cowgill
Pro Virtual Assistants, Inc.: Connie S. Hansen
REALPro Advantage: Sarah Rich
Remote Control: Kathi R. Hall
Sharper Listings: Kay W. Miller
Sherwood Group: Adrian D. Sherwood
Silent Partners Virtual Assistance Group: Ann Clubb
Stairs of Success: April Shockey
Synodyne: Christine Whitman
Texas Virtual Assistant Services: Rhonda Behnken
Tip Top Creations: Becky Holmes
Today's Online Concepts: Linda Compton
Ultimate Design Virtual Assistant: Delaine Ulmer
Valuable Connections: Laura Armbruster
Via Virtual Assistant, LLC.: Carole Gilmore
Virtual Assistance At Your Service: Margaret E. Doescher
Virtual Assistance of Houston: Shelly L. Fagin
Virtual Assistant On Demand: Suzanne Lee Ogle
Virtual Business Solutions: Lana Newlander
Virtual Dawn: Dawn E. Middlestead
Virtual Gal Friday: Nancy Brown
Virtual Jessica: Jessica Cano
Virtual Link, The: Anna Baron
Virtual Support Now: Linda Fleming
VMG-Virtual Assistants: Miki Von Luckner
Your Office 2: Meyosha Spencer
Web.Vir.Sist: Outsourcing Made Easy: Sonya Gray

Utah

AVA Virtual Services: Shirlee McGarry
Keystrokes: Julie Gubler

Vermont

Sarah Spencer Solutions, LLC: Sarah S. Spencer

Virginia

Alternative Virtual Solutions: Estela Rueda
Auxilium Virtual: Audrey Facemire
Brant Associates, A: Allison Brant
CVD Administrative Services, LLC: Carol Vodra Dodd

▲

Excellent Virtual Office Services: Deirdre Cooke
Executive Secretarial Services, LLC: Gay Lynn Kirsch
Gordon Business Solutions: Donna Gordon
Harmony Virtual Assistance: Kimberly J. Murray
J-Jireh Resources, LLC: Beverly Freeman
KLF and Associates: Kimberly L. Fairbanks
Letter Perfect Business Support: Antoinette D. Braswell
Olive Tree Consulting: Charlease R. Deathridge, SPHR
Patriotic Helping Hand: Mary Beth Gandee
Stacy Barrentine Event and Registration Services: Stacy Barrentine
Superb Support: Karen Axley
The Right Type: Erica M. Berrigan
Tidewater Mail and Business: Stephanie Finkbeiner
Valley Virtual Assistants: Heather Jacobson
Virtual Administrative Solutions: Lenore J. Daniels
Virtual Assistant Business Solutions: Heather K. Toth
Virtual Assist for Realtors: Chris Bragg
Virtually Yours...at the Lake: Claudia Davis
Virtual ProjectPoint: Christine Boran
Waivasir, Inc.: Kim R. Bloom
Yellow Highlighter Communication: Meredith Eisenberg
Your Home Office: Dawn Fowler
Your Virtual Office, Inc.: Paula H. Davis

Washington

Assist Virtually: Janet Edmiston Smith
BG & Associates Virtual Assistant Professionals: Barbara Alexander
Business Is Blooming!: Virtual Assistance & Professional Services: Tracee Chamberlain
Byte By Byte: Lisa Youngs
Digitalgybe: Your Virtual Back Office: Diane N. Ensey
Efficient Assistant: Karen White
Executive Solutions: Patti Bongers
Healer's Helper: Rita Ballard
KEV's Virtual Assistant Services: Kevin Valerio
Lady Of Letters, Inc.: Caren L. Trapp
LaRae's Virtual Assistance: LaRae McMullen
Microsoft Word Angel: Angelee Bivins
Moneypenny Assistants: Paula Williams
Precision Design Works: Sommer Ann Cronck
Reliable Cyber Solutions, LLC: Michele Wong

Schola Frisinger: Schola Frisinger
South Sound Lane Virtual Assistance: Dianna Giguere
TANDEM-Professional Business Virtual Assistance: Mariea A. Johnson
Type It: Tara Renick
Virtual Assistant In Demand: Lisa Y. Dixon
Virtual Solutions: Jodie Schanhals

West Virginia

Happy Fingers Word Processing & Business Services: Barbie Dallmann

Wisconsin

Abbydale Office Services: Merilyn C. Romani
Clark VA Solutions: Lori J. Clark
CWK Virtual Assistance, LLC: Mary Koch
E-Answers, LLC: Brenda Nickel
Executive Secretarial Services: Marsha Kopan
Laurie's Office Support: Laurie Lasee
MAD Typing and Consulting: Melanie A. O'Kane
Millane Virtual Assistants: Laurie Millane
Offsite Office Professionals, LLC: Deb Gonsalves
Prairie Business Partners: Gretchen Koehler-Swaney
Premier Administrative Services: Lisa Hoffman
REVA Online: Kathy Goldman
Swift Office Services, LLC: Yvonne T. McCoy
Thrive Outsourc,e LLC: Kimberly D. Cinnamon
Word Processing Plus: Sue Faris

Glossary

Autoresponder: A computer program that automatically answers email sent to it. They are often used as marketing tools to immediately reply to prospective clients notifying them that you will follow up at your earliest convenience.

COD, Cash on Delivery: a requirement that the cost of the service and/or product is paid at the time of delivery, used mostly when the sale is too small to warrant opening an account.

Corporation: a business structure organized under state law and generally treated as a separate tax entity.

CPA, Certified Public Accountant: a licensed accountant who has passed certain exams and fulfilled all of the requirements of his or her state in which they operate.

Data conversion: an altering of selected data for transfer from one program or format to another such as from a database file to a spreadsheet.

Data link: a connection between systems that allows information sharing such as a connection between documents with similar information that automatically updates all documents when one is changed.

Data management: the process of recording and manipulating data for business use.

DBA, Doing Business As: a qualifier that helps specifically identify a business entity when the business may be legally recorded under an individual or corporate name that helps the public better identify the product/service that they offer.

Deductions: business and other expenses that reduce your income.

Desktop publishing: the creation of graphics material such as newsletters, flyers, charts, etc.

Direct Marketing: typically used when selling by mail by addressing the sales material to a specific target market or group.

Employee Leasing Company: company that administers personnel functions for clients and "leasing" the client's employees back to them.

File maintenance: correcting and updating information in files and directories and removing outdated files for business use.

Flat rate: work done based on a fee agreed upon before a job is started, rather than by the hour.

Independent contractor: an individual who performs work on a contract basis and who is not an employee of the company for which he/she is doing the work.

Industry Production Standards (IPS): a method of measuring production output based on a "model operator" standard and used to calculate fees.

Limited Liability Company (LLC): a hybrid business structure that combines tax advantages of a partnership with the liability protection of a corporation.

Merchant account: an account that allows a business to accept credit card payments through their bank or directly from the credit card company.

Mission statement: a short written statement of your business goals and philosophies.

Notarize: to acknowledge or attest as a notary public.

Notary public: a public officer authorized to administer oaths, to attest to and certify certain types of documents, to take depositions, and to perform certain acts in commercial matters; also referred to as a notary.

Outsourcing: the business trend of contracting with outside suppliers to provide goods and services formerly produced in-house.

Rush rates: extra charges applied to work done in less time than your standard production period at the client's request.

Self-employment tax: tax paid by a self-employed person to help finance Social Security and Medicare.

Shareware: non-commercial software that's usually available on a trial basis.

Speech recognition technology: technology that allows a user to interface with a computer by speaking rather than by typing; also known as "voice recognition technology."

Sole proprietorship: a business owned by one person who has unlimited liability for the debts of the business.

Standard Industrial Classification (SIC) Code: a number used by the federal government to identify companies based on the product or service they provide.

Target market: the specific group of consumers or businesses you want to sell to.

Temporary employment company: company that recruits employees to work for client companies on a short-term basis.

Unique Selling Proposition (USP): what differentiates your service from others of a similar type and what makes it unique.

Video podcasting: A podcast is a media file which is distributed over the internet that is available for playback on PCs. Video podcasting is a specialized form involving video since podcasting was originally audio-based.

VoIP (Voice over Internet Protocol): a term for sending voice information in digital form over the internet. A major advantage of VoIP and internet telephony is that it avoids the tolls charged by ordinary telephone service.

Webcam: A video camera that is used to send periodic images or continuous frames to a web site for display. Webcam software typically captures the images as JPEG or MPEG files and makes them available for upload.

Whiteboard: a shared electronic workspace. Each participant can add text, make drawings or paste pictures on the whiteboard, and other participants can immediately see the result on their workstation. Each participant can make a printout of what was written or save it for later reference.

Index